T0361309

THE PAINTINGS IN
THE CNIDIAN LESCHE AT DELPHI
AND THEIR HISTORICAL
CONTEXT

MNEMOSYNE

BIBLIOTHECA CLASSICA BATAVA

COLLEGERUNT

A. D. LEEMAN · H. W. PLEKET · C. J. RUIJGH

BIBLIOTHECAE FASCICULOS EDENDOS CURAVIT

C. J. RUIJGH, KLASSIEK SEMINARIUM, OUDE TURFMARKT 129, AMSTERDAM

SUPPLEMENTUM SEXAGESIMUM OCTAVUM
OCTOGESIMUM

ROBERT B. KEBRIC

THE PAINTINGS IN THE CNIDIAN LESCHE AT DELPHI AND THEIR HISTORICAL CONTEXT

LUGDUNI BATAVORUM   E. J. BRILL   MCMLXXXIII

THE PAINTINGS IN
THE CNIDIAN LESCHE AT DELPHI
AND THEIR HISTORICAL
CONTEXT

BY

ROBERT B. KEBRIC

LEIDEN   E. J. BRILL   1983

ISBN 90 04 07020 6

PRINTED IN THE NETHERLANDS BY E. J. BRILL

For Judy

CONTENTS

ACKNOWLEDGMENTS

I would like to express my appreciation to Professors Verdenius, Janssen, and Boersma for their editorial assistance and comments. I would also like to thank Judith Kebric for her usual critical acumen in reviewing the various stages of the manuscript. Finally, I am grateful to the University of Louisville for its financial support in this project.

R.B.K.
Louisville, Kentucky
U.S.A.

THE PAINTINGS IN THE CNIDIAN LESCHE AT DELPHI
AND THEIR HISTORICAL CONTEXT

Two of the most famous paintings in antiquity were Polygnotus' *Il-iupersis* and *Nekyia*, commissioned by the Cnidians in the first half of the fifth century B.C. and housed in their Lesche at Delphi. So impressive were the murals, which depicted Troy fallen and Odysseus' visit to the Underworld, respectively, that Pausanias on his travels through Hellas in the second century A.D. felt compelled to describe them in minute detail, filling seven chapters in his section on Phocis (10.25-31).

The paintings were gigantic by contemporary standards—as may be surmised by the Lesche's 55′ × 25′ interior measurements—and their dozens of figures, arranged on at least three different levels on a surface perhaps 15′ high, approached but were somewhat less-than-life size.[1] While the murals have long since disappeared, there have been several attempts, mostly before this century, to reconstruct them in their entirety from Pausanias' description. Opinions as to the success of such efforts have been mixed, but the best known reconstruction, that of C. Robert,[2] who also provided lengthy commentary on the paintings, became the departure point for most succeeding scholarship, which has continued to contribute new ideas—artistic, archaeological, political, and his-torical—and to modify old ones about the Lesche and its paintings.[3] Nonetheless, the most important questions have remained largely unanswered. No one, for example, has been able to demonstrate satisfac-torily why the Lesche and its murals were originally set up. Suggestions have been offered, but, unsupported by careful analysis, they do not ad-vance the state of knowledge on the subject. A thorough examination into Cnidian activities both before and during the period in which the Lesche was constructed raises a number of pertinent points which heretofore have not been considered but are crucial in determining the precise motivation behind the dedication at Delphi. Delineating these points will be a major focus of the present study. There are also other important historical questions about the paintings which have not received adequate attention or need re-evaluation, and they, too, will be considered. The most pressing of these are why were the subjects of Troy fallen and Odysseus' visit to the Underworld chosen to adorn the interior walls of the Lesche; what political implications, if any, can be discerned in them; and why was Polygnotus selected as the artist for the project? The contention of this inquiry will be that the solution to these various questions concerning the Lesche and its murals lies in a single common denominator: the Athenian general Cimon's great victory over the Persians at the Eurymedon River. It will become clear how interrelated were the activities of Cimon with Cnidus, with the murals, and with Polygnotus, the artist who painted them. A discussion of the importance of the Eurymedon campaign to Cnidus and why the dedication of the Lesche and the paintings could only have been a consequence of that victory follows.

CHAPTER ONE

THE HISTORICAL CIRCUMSTANCES BEHIND THE LESCHE

While Aphrodite is the deity most associated with Cnidus, Apollo was also highly venerated, a fact re-emphasized in Cahn's recent study[4] and clearly demonstrated by the Cnidians' long-established ties with the god's shrine at Delphi, where they were particularly active. Among their more noteworthy contributions were a treasury (Paus. 10.11.5), erected ca. 550 B.C.; an even earlier dedication (ca. 570 B.C.) made by Cnidian colonists to the Lipari Islands (Paus. 10.11.3; Diod. 5.9.1ff.); and statues (Paus. 10.11.1) depicting Apollo and Artemis, their mother, Leto, and Triopas. The latter was the grandson of Apollo (Diod. 5.61.3) and, traditionally, the founder of Cnidus and neighboring Triopium,[5] where a major center of worship to Apollo was located.[6] With the Lesche and its paintings, however, the Cnidians had outdone themselves. This was definitely not the typical offering. Their previous dedications paled in comparison as did those of most other city-states, for this was a monument which would be unrivaled in the centuries to come. Located against the northern wall enclosing the uppermost part of the sacred precinct, the Lesche had a commanding and spectacular view of Delphi, overlooking the Temple of Apollo and the valley far below. It was perhaps the choicest location of any building within the precinct, and, as Pouilloux has already noted, the Lesche was not erected there by accident.[7] Archaeological work has revealed that a number of logistical problems caused by the uneven terrain had to be overcome before the edifice could be built; that, in itself, demonstrates a conscious effort to place the Lesche precisely where it was; the sanctuary was not so crowded that an alternative site could not have been found. One of the reasons for the building's privileged position was undoubtedly the favored status of the Cnidians in the eyes of Apollo. There were few people outside of Delphi who controlled as important a temple to the god as the Cnidians did,[8] and this certainly made the Delphians more receptive to them and their dedications. Another possible reason for the Lesche's location was that the tomb of the hero, Neoptolemus, was situated right below it. As will be seen (*infra*, pp. 22f.), Neoptolemus was a dominating figure in Polygnotus' *Iliupersis*; it would be remarkable if there were not some connection between that painting inside the Lesche and the hero's tomb. There may also have been technical advantages to placing the Lesche in the highest part of the precinct. Illuminating Polygnotus' paintings on the interior walls of the building would have been a major concern for the architects. How it was handled is not precisely known, but sunlight would have played an important role in any system.[9] Perhaps this site was chosen because the sun's rays could be utilized to the fullest advantage.

Since it is clear that the Lesche, or "Clubhouse," as it is frequently called, served primarily as a meeting place, this, too, must have been considered when its location was being determined. Pausanias (10.25.1) says that since early days, the Delphians had gathered there to discuss important matters and legendary topics; Plutarch, himself a priest of Apollo, has the participants in one of his dialogues (*De def. or.* 6) meet in the building. The Lesche seems always to have been a place where one could discuss politics or business, enjoy some lively conversation, or just relax and partake of the breath-taking view and some refreshment (Plutarch even associates it with athletic activity[10]). Visitors to the Temple of Apollo would find the "Clubhouse" only a short distance away and might pause there before beginning their homeward journeys; and, for that matter, any tourist, businessman, or citizen who found himself in the vicinity might duck in for a moment, whether to find relief from the summer heat and the formidable sloping paths of the precinct, or only to view the famous paintings. With the construction of the stadium on the heights above and, in the next century, the full development of the theater area close by, the Lesche must have, indeed, become a popular spot. While too little remains to reconstruct the building with accuracy,[11] certainly, it was designed to provide a pleasant atmosphere for its guests, and Polygnotus' murals no doubt contributed to that atmosphere. The Lesche, therefore, was a dedication which also had a utilitarian purpose, meant to serve the people of Delphi and their visitors, who were, on occasion, Cnidians. It was a gift for perpetuity, made clear by the fact that Cnidus continued to maintain the "Clubhouse" in the centuries to come.[12] Such magnanimity was unusual—even at Delphi. Offerings were expensive, made clear by Pausanias' comment (10.11.5f.) that they were usually the result of an important military victory, or a desire to display prosperity. To explain the Cnidians' dedication, one must look to their history during the first part of the fifth century B.C. for an event worthy of such commemoration (most assuredly accompanied by a dramatic increase in wealth). Fortunately, there was such an event: the battle at the Eurymedon River.

To fully understand the meaning of the victory at the Eurymedon for the Cnidians, a brief review of their experience with the Persians is necessary. According to Herodotus (1.174), the Cnidians fell under Persian suzerainty in the sixth century B.C. when Harpagus, Cyrus' general, was attacking Ionia.[13] They attempted to defend themselves by making Cnidus an island, digging a trench through the narrow neck of land which connected them to the mainland, but the work did not go well. Many were injured, mostly in the eyes, by flying fragments from the stones they hammered; and since the number of wounded was deemed far greater than might normally be expected, envoys were dispatched to Delphi to make an inquiry. There, they were told by Apollo that their work did not have Zeus' blessing, and that Cnidus was never meant to be separated from the mainland. Consequently, they abandoned the project. The Cnidians also must have interpreted Apollo's response to mean that they should give up their attempts to resist the Persians altogether for they submitted peacefully when Harpagus finally did arrive. This makes sense only if they felt that the god was, in fact, by his response, promising them that if they put their total faith in him, he would see them through the crisis. It was a "promise" on which Apollo did not renege: ultimately, he would safely deliver the Cnidians.

There is no reason to doubt the genuineness of Herodotus' account since the Cnidians, originally Dorians from the Peloponnesus,[14] were devoted to the Dorian Apollo. As mentioned previously, the god had an important center of worship in Triopium, and, certainly, the Cnidians would have consulted first the priests at the local shrine before taking their problem directly before the Delphic Apollo. Once they had received Apollo's answer, they decided to surrender, believing the god would protect them from harm. The fact that they had one of the god's "houses" so close at hand undoubtedly provided the extra confidence the Cnidians needed to pursue this course of action. They settled down into a role of subserviance under the Great Kings.[15]

Herodotus (3.138) makes it clear that, while under the rule of Darius, the Cnidians remained totally obedient to the King's commands. They were, however, allowed a certain amount of freedom; trade continued with other Greeks in the West, and Cnidus began to issue coinage, as Cahn has indicated.[16] Finally, the yoke was lifted sometime in the period subsequent to the Second Persian War, but the exact year remains a matter of debate. Diodorus (11.60.4), following Ephorus (*FGrH* 70 F191), says that prior to the pivotal battle at the Eurymedon (early 460's B.C.), the Athenian general Cimon sailed with his entire fleet along the Carian coast, persuading cities colonized from Greece to revolt, while subduing those with mixed populations and Persian garrisons. Plutarch (*Cim.* 12.1) is presumably referring to the same mission when he mentions that Cimon brought all the Asian coast from Ionia to Pamphylia under his control. But was Cnidus one of the cities liberated at this time? Gomme[17] does not think so, nor do Meritt, *et al.*,[18] who believe that Cnidus was, most likely, an original member of the Delian Confederacy, formed in 478/77 B.C.; Meiggs, while advising caution, appears to lean toward the same conclusion.[19] But even if Cnidus were not an original League member, there is evidence to suggest that it had become one before 472 B.C. The argument for this date rests primarily on an interpretation of a chorus from Aeschylus' *Persians* (852-906). In that chorus, the Persians recall the "better days" of Darius and recite a long list of Greek territories, including Cnidus, over which Xerxes' father ruled. The implication is that all these possessions were now in danger of being lost, and, if Aeschylus were attempting to heighten the dramatic irony of his play by having the chorus reflect upon areas his Greek audience knew *had already been taken from the Persians*, then the date of the performance, 472 B.C., can be used as a *terminus post quem* for the recovery of Cnidus and all the locations mentioned in the list. This, unfortunately, cannot be firm since there are strong arguments against Cyprus (included in Aeschylus' list), at least, being freed from Persian dominance during this period.[20]

A later date is suggested by Walker,[21] who believes that the whole of Caria except for Rhodes and some adjacent islands was retained by Persia until the Eurymedon campaign. This does not seem convincing—especially in the case of Cnidus, which must have been accessible to Cimon sometime before the battle ever took place. Plutarch (*Cim.* 12.2) states that the Athenian general sailed for the Eurymedon with 300 triremes from the double harbor of the Cnidians at Cnidus and nearby Triopium.[22] While Meiggs has raised some possible difficulties in Plutarch's account of Cimon's activities, they do not mitigate the basic observation that it was from Cnidus and Triopium that the final push toward the Eurymedon began.[23] Plutarch is very specific about this, and other considerations bear him out. Cimon's fleet was very large; there were only a few harbors on the southern coast of Asia Minor which could accommodate it. One immediately thinks of Rhodes, which was closer to the Eurymedon; but Cnidus offered two fine harbors, one right next to the other, and, also, it was more strategically situated. Rhodes was more vulnerable to a Persian naval attack, and, if besieged, could not be as easily reinforced as Cnidus. If the latter were assaulted unexpectedly, it could not only be supplied overland, but could also expect help from both Rhodes and the city-states of Ionia. Thus, logistically, Cnidus was better protected and more secure, advantages of which Cimon was very much aware since Plutarch indicates (*Cim.* 12.2) that it was here that the Athenian general chose to make extensive modifications on his ships in preparation for the Eurymedon.[24] The harbors at Cnidus may even have served as Cimon's base[25] of operations while he sailed the dangerous waters off Caria and Pamphylia. Whatever the case, Cimon *did* use the harbors, and that alone demonstrates that Cnidus was securely within the Delian fold before the battle of the Eurymedon ever took place.[26]

When Cimon defeated the Persians at the Eurymedon, Apollo's "promise," as interpreted by the Cnidians, was fulfilled. The god had brought them safely through difficult times and now rewarded their obedience and patience with freedom. What, then, would have been more appropriate at this time than to dedicate a special thank-offering to Apollo—an offering like the Lesche and its paintings. This idea, linking the Cnidian dedication with the Eurymedon victory, is not a new one.[27] Critics, however, would argue that since Cnidus, as indicated above, could have been free of Persian rule long before the battle took place, the triumph would not have had so much meaning for the Cnidians—certainly, not enough to prompt as magnificent an offering as the Lesche and its murals. But there is an important difference between a transitory freedom and actual deliverance; even if Cnidus were "freed" from Persia before Eurymedon, the situation remained precarious and unstable. The Cnidians could hardly have felt secure, and they were in no position to be making offerings at Delphi. What resources they did have undoubtedly went into bolstering their defenses. The victory at the Eurymedon changed all that. This was a crushing defeat for Persia which was so decisive that the fears of a Persian return all but disappeared. According to Callisthenes (*FGrH* 124 T 95e: Plut. *Cim.* 13.5), the effect was so great that, later, squadrons of fifty ships under Pericles and thirty under Ephialtes could sail as far as and beyond the Chelidonian Isles without ever seeing an enemy vessel. For the first time, the Cnidians could genuinely feel "delivered", and, for them, this deliverance was accentuated by the fact that Cimon's fleet had sailed for the Eurymedon from Cnidian harbors. Certainly, this was cause for "national" pride; but, more importantly, it was a sign that Apollo was personally orchestrating events: the very ships which won the final freedom for Cnidus set out from waters within sight of the god's temple at Triopium.[28] To the Cnidians, Apollo himself had dispatched the force which delivered them from Persian bondage, and the victory at the Eurymedon, in which they most assuredly participated (*infra*, p. 8), was the end of the cycle which had begun years before with their inquiry at Delphi.

The Cnidians could also see Apollo's presence in these events in another way. It must be remembered that the Eurymedon triumph was accomplished through the efforts of the Delian Confederation, to which Cnidus belonged. The League, of course, was headquartered on the island of Delos, traditionally the birthplace of the Ionian Apollo, and the latter was the patron deity of the Confederacy. Thus, Cimon, in his role as head of the Delian League, was, in essence, the agent of the god—a relationship which was physically represented in a statue group at Delphi (*infra*, pp. 25ff.)—carrying out Apollo's wishes at the battle of the Eurymedon River. Consequently, for the Cnidians, not only would they have felt that they had the Dorian Apollo securely on their side, but also the Ionian Apollo. Both had come together on this glorious occasion to inflict the greatest defeat ever visited by the Greeks upon the Persians, guaranteeing in the process the *final* liberation of Cnidus. The involvement of Apollo in these proceedings is, therefore, incontrovertible.

The victory at the Eurymedon *was* the event which prompted the dedication of the Lesche and its paintings. There simply is nothing else in Cnidian history which can explain the magnitude of the offering and which precisely fits the chronological limits for the Lesche's construction (second quarter of the fifth century B.C.[29]). There are other reasons to link the building and its murals with the Eurymedon—the most important of which are financial. Pausanias' statement about the cost of dedications at Delphi and the fact that they were affordable only if a city was unusually rich or had just won an important battle (and booty was plentiful) has already been mentioned. Most of the offerings seem to have fallen into the latter category. Thus, the Athenian treasury was built from the spoils of Marathon (Paus. 10.11.5); their portico was connected with the destruction of Xerxes' bridges over the Hellespont;[30a] their dedication to the Eurymedon victory (Paus. 10.15.4) from the spoils of that battle; the Theban treasury was funded by their triumph at Leuctra (10.11.5); the Syracusean treasury from the Athenian disaster of 413 B.C. (10.11.5). With their Lesche, however, the Cnidians do not appear to have been celebrating a victory so much as they were demonstrating their appreciation to Apollo (like the Potidaeans, who built their treasury to show their piety: 10.11.5). Nonetheless, it would have taken a huge sum of money to finance the project, and for that the triumph at the Eurymedon was very important. The spoils from the campaign were impressive, and scholars have spilled much ink postulating how many projects in the rebuilding and beautification of Athens were funded by them.[30b] Cnidus, too, would have taken its fair share of booty from the battle, and much of it (possibly all) would have gone for the dedication at Delphi. There can be no doubt that the Cnidians did participate in the actual fighting. They were members of the Delian League, and Cimon certainly would not have used their harbors and then left them behind. He needed all the help he could get, made clear by his experience with the Phaselians (Plut. *Cim.* 12.4), who, after initially rebuking him, accepted his terms of friendship—which included joining him at the Eurymedon. No such effort was needed to coax the Cnidians, who, as already mentioned, must have viewed the mission as "divinely-inspired". They would have mustered as many men and ships as they could. Evidence of a more substantial kind is not forthcoming. There is an inscription on a Hellenistic statue base from Samos which honors one Maiandrios' exploits at the Eurymedon,[31] but information about individual city-state's participation in the great battle does not extend much beyond this. It is amazing how inadequate and confused the sources are for one of the most significant triumphs in Greek history. Be that as it may, the Eurymedon provides a satisfactory answer not only for why the Lesche was erected, but also for where the funds came from to pay for it. Before the battle, Cnidus was weak and recovering from Persian rule; it could hardly have been financially solvent. As stated above, anything extra probably would have gone into defense. Whether it was in a position to contribute anything to the Delian League in the beginning cannot be known but ships are a strong possibility.[32] In the years after Eurymedon, however, there can be little doubt that Cnidus was paying an assessment, and assuredly, that assessment, whatever it was,[33] would have increased as the Athenian hold over members of the Confederation continued to tighten—especially after the abortive revolt of Thasos. Unfortunately, the earliest information from the *Athenian Tribute Lists* comes in 454/53 B.C., too late to be of any help;[34] but it seems reasonable to posit that Cnidus would have been less and less able to provide such a large outlay of money as would have been needed to finance their ambitious project at Delphi. Only in the short period directly following the Eurymedon victory would there have been the reason, the wealth, and the "autonomy" necessary to dedicate the Lesche and its paintings.

In order to pin down the date of the Lesche's construction more precisely, it is necessary to determine exactly when the battle of the Eurymedon took place. This is a difficult question, and there is little agreement on the specific year. Estimates range from 470/69-465 B.C.,[35] but a strong case may be argued for 469 B.C. It was first made by Jacoby,[36] reaffirmed forcefully by Meritt, *et al.*,[37] and has since continued to gain support.[38] The proposal is as follows: According to Plutarch (*Cim.* 8.7ff.), Cimon and his nine colleagues in the generalship were prevailed upon by the archon, Apsephion, to sit in judgment at the Dionysia in which Sophocles first competed against Aeschylus. Usually, the judges were selected by lot, and the fact that the ten generals presided over this competition made it very special. Since this was such a departure from the norm, Apsephion's action could be interpreted as a gesture to honor Cimon and his colleagues for some recent noteworthy achievement, grand enough to require the participation of all ten officers. Such an event was the battle of the Eurymedon. Therefore, since Apsephion was archon for 469/68 B.C. and the Dionysia took place in the Spring, 469 B.C. is the most likely date for the battle.

While the argument is ingenious, there remain several disturbing points. In the first place, Plutarch implies that Apsephion only turned to the generals because he feared the rivalry between the followers of Aeschylus and Sophocles. No matter who won, violence was certain to erupt. Furthermore, it appears that Apsephion did not decide to make Cimon and his fellow generals judges until after they had arrived at the theater. Even then, they were reluctant to take part, and Apsephion had to "twist a few arms" before they succumbed to his wishes. It is true that their role as judges did make this an unusual contest, one to be remembered, but very little of the account seems to support the interpretation that Apsephion meant to honor the generals by his action. Meiggs has recognised the problems and, while considering the case for 469 B.C. a "strong positive argument", finally concludes that Apsephion turned to the generals because of the "authority of their office"; it had nothing to do with the victory at the Eurymedon.[39]

Nevertheless, the argument for 469 B.C. cannot be dismissed so easily because Plutarch's account of the unusual episode is somewhat apocryphal. At this time Sophocles was the neophyte, Aeschylus, the master. It is only because one knows how famous Sophocles *will* become that the incident takes on its drama. Certainly, Sophocles, competing in his first Dionysia, could not possibly have had the following of the well-established Aeschylus who had a line of eight or nine successes by this time;[40] certainly, the tensions in this contest would not have been any greater than those which normally accompanied an important competition. Yet it was for this contest—and this one alone—that the ten generals were pressed into service as judges. If Apsephion really turned to them in hope of preventing violence, he would have set a memorable precedent. Why, then, is this the only instance? Athenian generals, as a rule, must have been present at the yearly Dionysias. Was there never again a situation in which a rivalry threatened violence? Was Apsephion the only archon with enough sense to turn to the generals to settle a disorderly crowd? Also, what were the advantages of making the generals judges? Was there any guarantee that their decision would not prompt rioting? Emotion does not always recognize rank. There are too many unanswered questions here to accept Plutarch's account as it stands. Furthermore, the ten officers were received by the restive crowd apparently without complaint, despite the unorthodox manner of their selection; and, Plutarch indicates that the judgment, which favored Sophocles,[41] was so popular that it—along with the return of the bones of Theseus—particularly endeared Cimon to the Athenian people. Both of these points are difficult to understand if the crowd were as partisan as Plutarch suggests. One would first have to accept that the unruly fans immediately turned docile in face of the generals' newly-acquired status as judges; and then, even if that were true, Aeschylus' supporters, ready to resort to fisticuffs only moments before, would have to have had a total change of heart if the decision for Sophocles was as popular as Plutarch says it was. In addition, Plutarch states that it was this decision which caused Aeschylus to become so angry that he moved to Sicily, where he eventually died. However, Aeschylus did not go to Sicily until sometime after the *Oresteia* was produced in 458 B.C.[42] It would have taken him ten years to become angry enough over his loss to leave town! In the meantime, he continued to garner dramatic victories.

This whole tradition, then, is suspect. The generals were not called upon to calm a hostile crowd. What appears to have happened is that later writers convinced themselves that the first competition between Aeschylus and Sophocles, two giants of the stage, *had* to have been a significant occasion; the fact that the generals were judges underscored its importance and justified the opinion that their presence was to insure that trouble did not break out. Thus, the story, casting the generals in the role of "crowd-controllers," came down to Plutarch. There had to be another reason why the generals were made judges, and the most logical is the one offered by Jacoby, *et al.*: Cimon and his colleagues *were*, indeed, being honored for an important service they had performed, and that service was, in all probability, their successful conclusion of the wars against Persia at the Eurymedon River—a victory of such magnitude and meaning (not to mention wealth) that it cut across all partisan lines[43] and demanded an appropriate show of public appreciation. Their unprecedented appointment as judges for the Dionysia of 468 B.C. by the archon, Apsephion, and their favorable reception by the crowd were signs of that appreciation. 469 B.C., then, remains the most "concrete" date for the battle at the Eurymedon, much more substantial than the chronological gymnastics employed in most other studies opting for a later date.

Connecting the Lesche and its paintings to the Eurymedon campaign in 469 B.C. necessitates a re-evaluation of the authenticity of the much-discussed epigram which appeared on the *Iliupersis* and was attributed by Pausanias (10.27.4) to Simonides. It runs as follows:

Polygnotus, the Thasian, son of Aglaophon,
painted Troy's citadel sacked.

There seems to be no question that there was an epigram on the painting; the debate rages over whether or not it may be attributed to

Simonides. Both sides of the controversy have had weighty advocates, but the issue remains unresolved.[44] There is really only one argument which can safely eliminate Simonides as the epigram's author—that he had died before the *Iliupersis* was ever commissioned. But if the battle of the Eurymedon did occur in 469 B.C., and the Cnidians began their Lesche soon after, Simonides, who lived until sometime in 468 B.C.,[45] could very well have composed the lines. He would have been in his late eighties and living in Sicily, but he needed neither to have seen the painting, nor to have lived through its completion to author the couplet. Some might argue that the epigram is undistinguished, not worthy of a Simonides; but how artistic could an old man be in two lines whose only purpose was to identify the artist, his origin, and the subject of his painting which was obvious? Still, none of this is absolutely convincing, and critics would cite numerous other epigrams which have been incorrectly attributed to Simonides, some, coincidentally, referring to the Eurymedon campaign.[46] But Simonides *could* have written the couplet (he wrote similar epigrams on the work of other prominent artists so it would not be an isolated incident—e.g. the doors painted by Dionysius of Colophon and Cimon of Cleonae[47]); Pausanias and the Delphians obviously thought he did; and, considering the fame of the painting and its artist, only an epigram by an equally famous poet would have been acceptable. The placing of a couplet by an unknown poet upon the *Iliupersis* would have been tantamount to defacing it.

A point which needs explanation if the epigram were *not* Simonides' is why there was no couplet accompanying the *Iliupersis'* sister painting in the Lesche, the *Nekyia*.[48] Was it not just as important to identify Polygnotus as the artist of this work? No one could automatically assume that since Polygnotus had done the *Iliupersis*, he was also responsible for the *Nekyia*. Projects of this sort were frequently the effort of more than one artist. And, if the epigram on the *Iliupersis* were composed by someone other than Simonides, why did he not also compose one for the *Nekyia*? It would have been just as simple to "forge" a second couplet. The most logical reason for the "omission" is that Simonides *did* compose the couplet for the *Iliupersis* but died before Polygnotus could begin work on the *Nekyia*. The *Iliupersis* was, in all probability, Polygnotus' first choice as a subject. It was the more impressive and famous of the two murals in the Lesche, and its theme was also the more popular one.[49] The latest evidence indicates that large murals of this sort were not painted directly on the wall surface but on wooden frames covered with boards which were pegged to the walls with iron pins.[50] Therefore, Polygnotus did not have to wait for the Lesche to be completed before beginning the *Iliupersis*. There can be no doubt that the building was originally designed to house the murals. They were much too large to have been added as an afterthought. Problems of displaying and lighting would have to have been worked out in advance. Polygnotus would have known the approximate size of the walls on which his paintings were to be mounted and could have started work before the building's foundation was even laid. Thus, even if Simonides did die sometime in 468 B.C., Polygnotus could already have been working a full year or longer on the *Iliupersis*. The epigram appeared on the last panel of the painting described by Pausanias, but, depending on how one chose to view it, that same panel could just as easily have been the first one—where Polygnotus began. Consequently, the couplet could have been on the earliest part of the *Iliupersis*, painted shortly after the battle of the Eurymedon at a time when Simonides was still alive. How long it would have taken the artist to complete his mural is a matter of conjecture, but, certainly, Simonides had died before it was finished. When Polygnotus began the *Nekyia*, the poet had already composed his last epigram; hence, none appears on the latter painting. (Some might argue that if Simonides were alive when the *Iliupersis* was being painted, then he also would have been able to provide a couplet for the *Nekyia*. However, there is no way of knowing whether Polygnotus had decided upon a theme for the second painting until later; but even if he had, there is no reason to suspect that couplets would have been composed for both paintings at the same time: neither Simonides nor Polygnotus knew when the former would die, and, as far as anyone did know, Simonides would be available to furnish an epigram for the second painting whenever it was requested (it would not be the first case of a lack of human foresight). Furthermore, Simonides himself may have refused to author a couplet until he knew that work had actually begun on the *Nekyia*; otherwise, if Polygnotus changed his mind, there would have been an epigram of his circulating which identified a non-existent painting.)

In sum, there was no time during the second quarter of the fifth century B.C. that the Cnidians would have had the reason, the funds, and the "autonomy" to dedicate the Lesche and its paintings at Delphi except in the period directly following the battle of the Eurymedon. The best estimate for that battle is 469 B.C., and, this being the case, the disputed epigram which appeared on the *Iliupersis* could have been and, in all probability, was the work of Simonides.

CHAPTER TWO

THE THEMES AND THE POLITICAL IMPLICATIONS
OF THE LESCHE'S PAINTINGS

The choice of themes related to the Trojan Cycle for the paintings in the Cnidian Lesche at Delphi was not an original one—Cleanthes of Corinth, for example, had already painted an *Iliupersis* in the temple of Artemis *Alpheionia* in Pisa near Olympia (Plin. *NH* 35.15f.; Strab. 8.343; Athen. 8.346BC), and the "Kleophrades Painter" had employed the same theme on a vase before 470 B.C.[51]—but neither was the choice a capricious one. The effort and expense that went into completing the giant *Iliupersis* and *Nekyia* in the Lesche make it unlikely that they were meant to be purely cosmetic, ornamental with no symbolic meaning. The murals were, after all, located at Delphi, a shrine for all Greeks, and the Trojan War was their common heritage. The Cnidians held strongly to that same tradition—their distant past could be directly linked to the great conflict itself since Nireus, the king of Syme who fought with Agamemnon at Troy (*Il.* 2.671ff.), was also ruler over a part of the Cnidia in the earliest days (Diod. 5.53.1f.)—but for over a half-century they had lived under the shadow of their Persian overlords. Consequently, at the first opportunity after regaining their freedom, it would have been appropriate for them to reaffirm their "Greekness," if for no other reason than to allay any suspicions about their loyalty and patriotism during the Persian occupation. Some Greeks certainly must have wondered about them, considering how willingly they had appeared to go over to the enemy. It was important, therefore, for the Cnidians to emphasize and celebrate the role Apollo had played in determining past events. The Lesche and its paintings were a step in the right direction.

But themes from the Trojan Cycle, particularly that of the *Iliupersis*, may also reflect directly upon the great victory at the Eurymedon River, in which the Cnidians, themselves, must have participated (*supra*, p. 8). It is clear from Herodotus, who lived through the period under discussion, that many Greeks, himself included, regarded the wars with Persia not as a series of random engagements but as part of an ongoing East-West struggle which had begun with the Trojan War. There can be no question about this as Herodotus (1.4) relates the Persians' version of how the conflict began:

> "... the Greeks, for the sake of a woman from Lacedaemon, assembled a great army, invaded Asia, and destroyed the kingdom of Priam. Ever since that day, we have considered the Greeks our enemies."

This view that the Persian Wars were an extension of the Trojan War was undoubtedly also responsible for passages like one found in Plutarch's life of *Agesilaus*. The Spartan king, who led an expedition against Persia in the early fourth century, is cast in the role of a latter-day Agamemnon. As he slept at Aulis on the eve of his departure, a voice came to him in a dream:

> "King of the Lacedaemonians, surely you know that no one has ever been made general over all Hellas save Agamemnon in former times and, now, you. Since you command the same army, war against the same enemy, and depart from the same place, it is only appropriate that you should offer the goddess the same sacrifice Agamemnon made before he sailed (*Ages.* 6.4)."

Cimon's struggle with the Persians was specifically compared with the conflict at Troy. Plutarch (*Cim.* 7.1-8.1) states that the Athenians allowed Cimon to set up three "Hermae" to celebrate his victory at Eion,[52] and the third of these dedications was inscribed with the lines:

> "Once from this city, together with the Atridae, Menestheus
>   Led his men to the divine plain of Troy.
> He, as Homer declared, of the well-armored Greeks,
>   Was best of all who had come in marshalling forces in battle.
> Thus, there is nothing unseemly in calling the Athenians
>   Leaders both for their skill in war and their manly courage."[53]

The battle of the Eurymedon would have been seen by many Greeks as another episode in the continuing conflict between East and West; and, with Cimon's victory there, another "Trojan War" had come to an end. Comparisons with the earlier heroics at Troy were unavoidable since this triumph also had occurred in Asia, and the magnitude of the victory was unparalleled since the days of Achilles and Agamemnon. Marathon, Salamis, Plataea, Mycale—none could compare,[54] and, as at Ilium, there was a certain finality about Eurymedon. With the Greeks of Asia Minor freed, the Aegean made a "Greek lake," and the Persians in retreat, the Greeks may have thought that the years of conflict with Asia were finally over and a new era was beginning. Cimon, an experienced propagandist, having exploited the heroic past for personal aggrandizement, i.e. Theseus,[55] would have recognized the benefits of fostering any parallels possible between his victory and the one at Troy; undoubtedly, he would have encouraged such, as well as any project which related in some way to the Eurymedon. Thus, it is very probable that his hand was at work, directly or indirectly, in the Cnidian Lesche (a type of building Pausanias (10.25.1) identifies with Homeric days) and its paintings, which must be regarded as "by-products" of the latest "Trojan War." Undeniably, Cimon could exercise a great influence over the Cnidians as the "agent" of Apollo who "delivered" them at the Eurymedon and as head of the Delian League to which Cnidus belonged. If there were any single figure to whom the Cnidians had to answer, it was Cimon. During the same years, he was also extremely influential at Delphi,[56] where the Athenians had set up a monument to his victory at the Eurymedon (Paus. 10.15.4; Plut. *Nic.* 13.3; *De Pyth. or.* 8; *Quaest. conv.* 724B). Consequently, Cimon's special influence at both Cnidus and Delphi in the 460's together with paintings whose themes can relate to his victory at the Eurymedon (the *Iliupersis*, for instance, does show Troy fallen, the same finality which characterized the "fall of Troy" at the Eurymedon) is sufficient reason to suspect some connection between the Cnidian dedication and Cimon. It would be appropriate to examine the details of the *Iliupersis* and also the *Nekyia* to see what relation, if any, they might bear to Cimon. There have already been a number of attempts to read specific political implications into portions of the paintings, and it might be well to review them first.

In the last century, Robert thought that Polygnotus' omission in the *Nekyia* of three of four Theban women Homer says Odysseus saw in the Underworld was a deliberate attempt to slight Thebes. He concluded that the explanation lay in the fact that the Thebans were bitter enemies of the Phocians, and that the latter controlled Delphi from 458-447 B.C.[57] The painting, therefore, must have been executed while Phocis dominated the shrine. Despite Frazer's rejection of this interpretation (if correct, why include any Theban women?),[58] Klein supported Robert, citing the prominence of Phocian heroes in both the *Nekyia* and the *Iliupersis*.[59] Weickert later anwered him with the reminder that this was a Cnidian dedication—not a Phocian one—also rejecting the date of 458-447 B.C. in favor of 469 B.C. or before.[60] C. Dugas, who has looked at the political implications of the figures perhaps closer than anyone, thought he saw a definite "Dorian" flavor given to the paintings, especially the *Iliupersis*.[61] This was done, he concluded, at the expense of Athens. Thus, there is the prominence of Helen, the wife of Menelaus; the replacement of the more popular motif of the flight of Aeneas' family with that of Antenor's—the latter being a friend of Menelaus and whose sons shipwrecked on Crete, friendly with Cnidus; and the presence of Neoptolemus, whose cruelty at Troy would later be punished by Apollo (a Dorian god also prominent at Triopium in Cnidus), or who, according to another Dorian version of the story, would be killed by Orestes, Menelaus' nephew. All this Dugas believes was calculated to please the Cnidians, emphasizing their Dorian background. How was Athens slighted? Dugas believes this can be seen primarily in the figure of Aethra, Theseus' mother, who is portrayed still in a state of bondage to

Helen. Her grandson, Demophon, is entirely dependent upon the generosity of the Spartan queen to win his grandmother's release. Consequently, Athens (i.e. the figures of Aethra and Demophon) has been assigned a noticeably subserviant role in this very pro-Dorian scene. While Dugas' arguments have been generally accepted,[62] there is, in fact, very little to recommend them. His interpretation of the figures is somewhat simplistic and fails to consider thoroughly the variant traditions associated with them which might undermine his thesis. Each of his points may be successfully neutralized.

As for the idea that the *Iliupersis* reflects poorly on family members of Theseus and, thereby, on Athens, the figure of Laodice, one of the Trojan women, is especially noteworthy. According to one story (Parth. *Amat. Narr.* 16), she fell in love with Acamas, the son of Theseus, and bore him a child. Another version of the account (Plut. *Thes.* 34.1) substitutes Theseus' son, Demophon, for Acamas. Both Acamas and Demophon are pictured in the *Iliupersis*, and Demophon, as mentioned previously, is one of the very figures Dugas wants to use to demonstrate his anti-Athenian thesis. Pausanias (10.26.7f.), however, following Homer, identifies Laodice as the wife of Antenor's son, Helicaon. Antenor and some members of his family—but *not* Helicaon—are also included in the painting, and Dugas, as will be remembered, views Antenor's presence as a sign of pro-Dorianism. If Dugas' interpretation is correct, anyone looking at the *Iliupersis* who was familiar with Laodice's connections with both Antenor's and Theseus' family would have been confused. Here was a painting in which Laodice was present, but her husband, Helicaon, absent. This being the case, one would naturally expect to find Laodice pictured with her husband's family, preparing to leave. She is not. In fact, she is in the same vicinity of the painting as Theseus' son, Acamas, who by one tradition was her lover and father of her child. Furthermore, Demophon, the other son of Theseus,[63] who is attributed the same role as Acamas by the second tradition, appears in another portion of the *Iliupersis* with his grandmother, Aethra (*supra*), who cared for Laodice's illicit child. Possibly, this situation can be interpreted in more than one way, but there is little to suggest that it could be complimentary to Antenor and his family. An unfaithful daughter-in-law depicted in the same painting as the family she betrayed while her lovers by two different traditions, sons of Theseus, and their grandmother are close at hand hardly seems an appropriate way to express pro-Dorianism. Moreover, as Robertson has correctly pointed out, among the Greeks Antenor was regarded as a traitor.[64] Polygnotus appears to have been representing him as such in the *Iliupersis* since he painted the leopard's skin, a sign to the Greeks to leave

Antenor's house alone, still hanging over the doorway as the Trojan and his family prepare to leave (Paus. 10.27.3). There is also little to support the contention that Polygnotus was showing a Dorian preference when he substituted the flight of Antenor's family for the better-known flight of Aeneas and his household. Traditionally, Aeneas had escaped during the night, before the city had fallen. In the process, he left behind his wife, usually identified as Creusa; and, logically enough, there is a woman by that name represented among the captive Trojan Women. It seems clear that in Polygnotus' mind, Aeneas had already left. For these reasons, it is incomprehensible how the painting could, in any way, favor Antenor and his family. (Also, since one of Antenor's sons was named Acamas, the presence in the *Iliupersis* of Theseus' son by the same name, the man who had corrupted the wife of Acamas' brother, Helicaon, would have provided, if anything, a touch of pro-Athenian irony.) Thus, the dangers of trying to interpret individual figures or groups of figures in the paintings in political terms becomes immediately apparent. Nonetheless, if one *were* to make a political case for the murals, it would certainly tend to favor a pro-Athenian rather than a pro-Dorian sentiment. This can be demonstrated by again using Laodice as an example.

Pausanias admits he is somewhat confused to discover Laodice in the *Iliupersis* since he cannot find her name in any poet's list of Trojan captive women. Therefore, he theorizes she must have been set free by the Greeks (10.26.7). Pausanias' confusion is good indication that one might not expect to find Laodice in the painting, at least in the way she is pictured. According to the most prominent story, she was swallowed up by the earth when Troy fell. Consequently, it seems that Polygnotus was exercising a bit of artistic license when he included the woman regarded by Homer (*Il.* 3.121ff.) as the most beautiful of Priam's daughters. But was beauty alone the reason Polygnotus made room for Laodice? Possibly, her presence can be interpreted as a reflection of pro-Athenian, and more specifically, pro-Cimonian sentiment. It has already been noted that different stories make Laodice the consort of either Acamas or Demophon, Theseus' sons. This by itself connects her firmly with Athenian tradition, but there is more. At Athens in the Stoa Poikile, Polygnotus painted a second and smaller version of the *Iliupersis* (Paus. 1.15.2; Plut. *Cim.* 4.5f.). He could have reproduced any part of the larger Delphic painting at Athens, yet he chose that portion of the mural which included Laodice, the very figure whose presence had troubled Pausanias. In the Athenian painting, Laodice was given a prominent place, made clear by the fact that Polygnotus painted her face in the image of his girlfriend, Elpinice (Plut. *Cim.* 4.5f.). Elpinice was also the sister of Cimon, and other evidence makes it clear that Polygnotus had been a member of Cimon's

circle for some time before he painted in the Stoa, which had been completed by ca. 460 B.C. (*infra*, pp. 33ff.).[65] Thus, the artist's free interpretation of Laodice's features may have been more than just empty self-
indulgence.[66] Whatever the case, the figure of Laodice *does* appear in
both the Delphic and the Athenian paintings, and, considering her ties
with Theseus' family, this does not appear to be happenstance; rather it
suggests that she was meant to represent pro-Athenian, and more particularly, a pro-Cimonian sentiment. This is further indicated by the
building in which Polygnotus painted Laodice for the second time, the
Stoa Poikile. The destruction of Athens by the Persians in 479 B.C. had
left the city in ruins and provided Cimon the opportunity to establish his
name as a builder as well as a general. His tenure in office was marked by
extensive building and beautification projects as Plutarch (*Cim.* 13. 6f.)
notes, and modern scholars have made, rightly or wrongly, everything
from the great statue of Athena Promachus on the Acropolis to the
Hephaesteum his responsibility.[67] Much of this rebuilding could not have
been realized without the funds that came from the spoils of the
Eurymedon (*supra*, p. 8); consequently, a large part of the reconstruction which took place during this period was, indirectly, another monument to Cimon's great victory. The Stoa Poikile, originally known as the
"Peisianakteion," was certainly a product of these days, built by a man
whom Davies and most others identify as Cimon's brother-in-law.[68]

The "Cimonian" atmosphere surrounding the Stoa has been
mentioned frequently;[69] inside there were murals, besides the one containing Laodice, which related directly to Theseus, the hero to whom
Cimon owed so much of his political success, and Cimon's own family
(*infra*, pp. 35f.). Thus, Laodice, the lover of Theseus' son (Acamas or
Demophon), reappears in Athens in a scene similar to the one at Delphi
in a "Cimonian" building with "Thesean" and "Cimonian" murals.
The artist in both cases was Polygnotus, Cimon's friend and associate. It
is almost impossible, therefore, to view Laodice as anything other than
an Athenian symbol in both paintings, and Dugas' theory of pro-
Dorianism, anti-Athenianism in the *Iliupersis* at Delphi is further under-
mined. In addition, another part of the Athenian *Iliupersis* included the
figures of the Lesser Ajax and the "kings" who had gathered to witness
his oath, a consequence of his outrage upon Cassandra and the shrine of
Athena. While Pausanias' description (1.15.1ff.) lacks detail, it is clear
that Polygnotus had reproduced in his Athenian painting that same portion of the Delphic *Iliupersis* which was adjacent to Laodice—the oath of
Ajax. The kings mentioned by Pausanias in the scene at Delphi were
Odysseus, Agamemnon, and Menelaus,[70] and there is no reason to
believe that they were not the same kings in the Athenian painting. If

Dugas' theory is correct, one of these kings, Menelaus, would have to be regarded as a pro-Dorian, anti-Athenian figure. Consequently, the Athenians would have to have been degrading themselves by including him in their *Iliupersis*.

The Athenian version of Ajax's oath undoubtedly also included among its figures Acamas, Theseus' son, and his friend, Polypoetes, the son of Theseus' close friend, Peirithous. In the painting at Delphi, Acamas and Polypoetes were definitely a part of the assemblage gathered around Ajax. They were positioned next to Odysseus, who stood near Ajax himself, and Pausanias indicates (10.26.2f.) that Acamas is wearing a helmet similar to the kind sported by Agamemnon and Menelaus. It would have made no sense at all for Polygnotus to exclude Theseus' son—an Athenian tribe was named after him—and his friend, whose father was so close to Theseus, from the Athenian *Iliupersis*; the presence of Laodice, Acamas' lover, in that same painting and the general "Thesean" flavor of the Stoa Poikile's murals (*infra*, pp. 35f.) are additional guarantees of the two's inclusion. Therefore, the mural in Athens, like the one at Delphi, must have contained Acamas,[71] his lover, Laodice, and his friend, Polypoetes. Athena was also represented in strong terms since Ajax, by his oath, was repenting not only his outrage upon Cassandra, but also, and more importantly, his defilement of the Athenian goddess' image and sanctuary. The figure of Agamemnon in the same scene might also have evoked consciously or unconsciously, some thought of Cimon since he was the "new" Agamemnon. In most respects, then, the *Iliupersis* at Athens appears to have been a reproduction[72] of a section—the central section[73]—of the *Iliupersis* at Delphi. With so many pro-Athenian figures in it, the subject matter could not have been random, and, if the Athenian mural celebrated Athens and her heroes, how could the Delphic painting, by the same artist and colleague of Cimon, not? Even if there were *no* picture in Athens and this section of the Delphic *Iliupersis* were viewed in isolation, a pro-Athenian sentiment prevails.

The fact that the presence of Acamas and Polypoetes together in the *Iliupersis* at Delphi is complimented by the appearance of their fathers, Theseus and Peirithous,[74] together in the *Nekyia* is another point Dugas should have noted. Like their sons, Theseus and Peirithous are also pictured close to Odysseus, who, in this painting, is summoning up spirits from the Underworld. This scene constitutes the focal point of the painting; thus, Theseus and Peirithous are central to the mural just as their sons were in the *Iliupersis*. But exactly how they are portrayed is not entirely clear from Pausanias' description. They are sitting on chairs, Theseus holding both his sword and his friend's, while Peirithous looks at the weapons, perhaps silently cursing their uselessness in preventing capture and confinement by Hades. According to the tradition, they had gone down into the Underworld with the purpose of carrying off Persephone to make her Peirithous' wife, but Hades thwarted their effort by inviting them to sit in chairs of forgetfulness that would hold them forever. One story indicates that chains confined them in the chairs; another, that rock grew to their flesh. There is no way to discern from Pausanias' account in which fashion, if either, Polygnotus represented the two, but one would have expected Pausanias to note specifically how they were depicted if there were something distinctive about their situation. He only states that they are "sitting on chairs" (ἐπί θρόνων καθεζόμενοι), and, if this were the case, then Polygnotus represented them in a less humiliating fashion. Consequently, the artist might have been expressing some pro-Athenian sentiment: Tradition dictated the general way in which Theseus and his friend had to appear in the Underworld—that could not be changed; but Polygnotus could manipulate details to present the two in the most flattering way, i.e. without chains or without rock growing to their flesh. There is no doubt that Theseus and Peirithous were treated sympathetically in the *Nekyia*,[75] and viewers knew that Theseus, at least, had been placed in the unenviable position of having to offend Hades in order to remain loyal to an oath he had made before Zeus. That oath compelled the hero to accompany Peirithous to the Underworld to carry off Persephone.[76] Consequently, no matter what Theseus did, trouble at the hands of one of the gods was sure to ensue. He chose to honor his oath and help his friend, and, considering the alternative—angering Zeus and Peirithous—this was not an ignoble choice. The friendship of Theseus and Peirithous was proverbial, and even the *Nekyia* conjured up a positive image of it, made clear by Pausanias' own reaction when he saw the two together in the Underworld. He launched into a short digression on their famous relationship (10.29.10), quoting laudatory passages about them from both the *Iliad* and the *Odyssey*, the latter of which is particularly noteworthy. Odysseus, while on his visit to the fringes of the Underworld, laments the fact that he has not time to see great men of an earlier day and refers specifically to Theseus and Peirithous, whom he calls "the glorious heroes of the gods" (*Od.* 11.631). It has already been noted that in Polygnotus' painting Theseus and Peirithous are pictured just below Odysseus—anyone who was familiar with Odysseus' opinion of the two (Pausanias was) would have seen a positive relationship being expressed here. Add to this the fact that Pausanias felt Polygnotus based his characterization of Charon, the ferryman, on the experience that Theseus and Peirithous had with him in a poem called the *Minyad* (10.28.2)—so it would seem that, to some degree, Polygnotus was using the two heroes' exploits as a guide toward portraying certain other scenes in the *Nekyia*—and the suggestion that the artist regarded the two friends in a positive way continues to grow. Certainly, Polygnotus meant to suggest some relationship between the fathers in the *Nekyia* and their sons in the *Iliupersis*; otherwise, there was no pressing reason to include Acamas and Polypoetes in the scene of Ajax's oath, which, as Robertson has pointed out,[77] was a rather obscure tradition, and the two certainly were not of much importance for their actions at Troy. If this were a pro-Dorian painting, one wonders why they would have been included at all; but they *are*, and because their fathers, one of whom is the greatest Athenian hero, are in the *Nekyia*, it is difficult not to see pro-Athenian sentiment here.

The most important thing to demonstrate about the scene in which Theseus and Peirithous appear is that there is no pro-Dorian slant given to their portrayal—certainly, this was a situation which could have been exploited to illustrate anti-Athenianism: Since the helpless Theseus was ultimately saved by Heracles, a Dorian hero, Polygnotus certainly would not have been serving his Dorian paymasters well by passing over such an obvious opportunity to display pro-Dorianism. Yet Heracles does not even appear in the painting, and, as noted above, there is no proof that Theseus and his friend are represented in an undignified manner—chained or held by rock. They appear close to Odysseus, whose feelings toward them are clearly positive; both Theseus and Peirithous are presented sympathetically; and Theseus, at least, was in this predicament only because he valued the meaning of his oath (it is interesting that an oath is the motivating factor behind both of the scenes in which the fathers and the sons appear). Lastly, it appears that Polygnotus depended somewhat on a poetic account which followed closely the exploits of the two heroes in the Underworld for his depiction of other figures in the *Nekyia*.

Finally, there are Dugas' observations about Neoptolemus and Helen. As will be remembered, he associated Neoptolemus with pro-Dorianism because he would ultimately be punished by Apollo, a Dorian god, or be killed by Orestes, nephew of Menelaus (*supra*, p. 16). How all this may be gleaned from the painting is not entirely clear since there does not appear to be *any* conscious effort on Polygnotus' part to visually represent the impending doom of Neoptolemus. In the *Iliupersis*, he was portrayed as the only Greek still killing Trojans, and, certainly, if Polygnotus had wished to display Apollo's displeasure with Neoptolemus, he could have found a less obscure way to do it—he had not been so subtle in his treatment of the Lesser Ajax's sacrilege! Apollo was also responsible for the death of Neoptolemus' father, Achilles, guiding the arrow that killed him (in punishment for slaying his son, Tenes). Achilles was represented in the *Nekyia*, and, if as Dugas suggests the paintings were concerned with expressing Apollo's wrath, one would expect to find some indication of the god's displeasure with him also. Nothing obvious emerges, and Dugas is left with the task of explaining why the scene with Neoptolemus would consciously evoke reminders of Apollo's wrath while the one containing Achilles does not—even though both had committed "crimes" against the god.[78] Dugas' alternative suggestion that Orestes was responsible for Neoptolemus' death and, thereby, represented pro-Dorianism is equally weak because the most plausible explanation for the prominence of Neoptolemus in the *Iliupersis* is given by Pausanias, himself. He relates (10.24.6) that the Delphians sacrificed to Neoptolemus as a hero every year and that Polygnotus meant for the son of Achilles to have a central position in the painting because the former's tomb was located just below the Cnidian Lesche (10.26.4). His depiction as still fighting is more out of respect for this fact than anything else. Poulsen[79] echoes these thoughts, as does Robertson, who states that Pausanias must have regarded the Lesche as devoted in some sense to Neoptolemus and that Polygnotus wanted to represent the hero in his traditional role as a "firebrand."[80]

Concerning Helen, Dugas views her presence in the *Iliupersis* as dominate and perhaps the purest indication of his pro-Dorian thesis. She is pictured with Theseus' mother Aethra, who is still in a state of bondage, while Theseus' son, Demophon, waits close by to rescue his grandmother. Pausanias (10.25.8) relates a story which states that when Troy fell, Aethra made her way into the Greek camp and was recognized by Theseus' sons. Demophon then asked Agamemnon to free her, but the Greek commander said that first Helen, whose handmaiden Aethra was, had to give her consent. Dugas accepts Pausanias' story as accurately reflecting the details behind the events pictured in the painting and interprets the fact that the decision to release Aethra rests ultimately with Helen as a sign of pro-Dorianism: the Athenian (or Thesean) figures, Aethra and Demophon, are at the mercy of the wife of Menelaus, and, thereby, the supremacy of the Dorian figure is established. The scene could be interpreted as being derogatory to Athens only if Demophon had to humiliate himself by begging for the release of his grandmother. It is clear from Pausanias' story that this was not the case. When Demophon learned of his grandmother's presence, he took the matter, as might be expected, to his commander-in-chief and requested her release. Agamemnon was sympathetic but was also respectful of Helen's position as wife of his brother and queen of Sparta. This seems clear from the fact that Agamemnon kept the matter on an *official* level by sending his own herald, Eurybates, pictured next to Helen in the *Iliupersis*, to convey his thoughts. Once they became known, Helen released Aethra. In all this, there is nothing to suggest, as Dugas believes, that Demophon had been subordinated to Helen. In addition, Demophon need not be regarded as a passive figure. One story, in fact, states that he demanded, not requested, the release of his grandmother from Agamemnon, and Pausanias' description (10.25.7) of his attitude in the painting gives the impression he is ready to take whatever measures are necessary to rescue Aethra—no matter what Helen decided. Helen originally seems to have made Aethra her handmaiden in revenge for Theseus' rape while she was a young girl. There is no indication, however, that after carrying Helen off with Peirithous, Theseus never mistreated her (that was not the reason the hero and his friend ended up in the Underworld—the entire affair relates only indirectly to their predicament); in fact, reluctant to offend the Dioscuri, he sent her away to be reared with the greatest care by his friend, Aphidnus. Aethra accompanied Helen and behaved as a mother toward her. In return, Helen enslaved and abused Aethra, whose appearance with shaven head in the *Iliupersis* certainly cannot be regarded as a sign of good will! One could easily read the scene as that of a humiliated old woman and mother of noble background, detained and abused by a vengeful Spartan queen. Helen would, thereby, seem a rather dislikeable figure, while the sympathy would rest with Aethra and her loyal grandson, who was trying to rescue her.[81] Even Agamemnon, commander-in-chief of the Greeks, is on the side of the pro-Thesean, pro-Athenian characters as evidenced by the presence of his messenger conveying his wishes to Helen. Interestingly, in the same period that the *Iliupersis* was painted, the "Anakeion," or sanctuary of the Dioscuri, in which Polygnotus also painted, was being built (or restored) under the auspices of Cimon in Athens (*infra*, p. 35). Consequently, if Dugas is correct, at the same time anti-Athenianism was being expressed through Helen in the Delphic mural, pro-Dorianism was exhibited through the celebration of her brothers in Athens by Cimon, the contemporary figure who was most associated with Theseus (and, thereby, Aethra). The pro-Dorian and anti-Athenianism which Dugas would like to see in the scene with Helen, Aethra, and Demophon cannot be substantiated, and a pro-Athenian, anti-Dorian interpretation is just as viable a suggestion.

No consistent pattern of pro-Dorianism can be found in the paintings; in fact, no individual case of pro-Dorianism can be substantiated. Furthermore, if the murals were, in fact, designed to celebrate Cnidus, the omission of Nireus (*supra*, p. 14), who ruled a portion of the Cnidia and who was the Cnidians' *only* direct link with the Trojan War, is incomprehensible. Where arguments can be made, a pro-Athenian, pro-Cimonian sentiment has emerged, and the following observations further support this idea. In the *Nekyia*, the sisters of Ariadne and Phaedra, wives of Theseus at different times (Phaedra was the mother of Acamas), are pictured together—not far from Theseus (Paus. 10.29.3f.). Their relationship to Theseus by itself marks them as pro-Athenian characters, but there is more. Phaedra is pictured on a swing which Pausanias interprets as an allusion to her death by hanging. Robertson[82] suggests that here Polygnotus may have been thinking of the Athenian festival, *Anthesteria*, which included a swinging ritual. This supposedly recalled the death of Erigone, who hung herself after offending Dionysus. As another contradiction to the pro-Dorian arguments, one wonders why Phrontis would have been pictured as pilot of Menelaus' ship in the *Iliupersis* since he had a permanent connection with Athens. In the *Odyssey* (3.276ff.), he was killed (by the arrows of Apollo, no less) and buried near Sounion in Attica. As Robertson has pointed out,[83] the Athenians honored his grave, and by the time the paintings in the Lesche were executed, he would certainly have been associated by most people with Athens. The Lesser Ajax provides an additional indication of pro-Athenianism, though an indirect one. Polygnotus had pictured Ajax in the *Iliupersis*, but he also painted him into the *Nekyia* (Paus. 10.31.1ff.). In the latter painting, Ajax's appearance is quite revealing. He is shown as a drowned sailor, covered with brine—the direct result of Athena's revenge for his outrage against her shrine and Cassandra. No one who viewed this pitiful figure in the mural could forget that Athena, the patron goddess of Athens, was responsible for his demise. Finally, Robertson has identified a chorus in Aeschylus' *Seven Against Thebes* (854ff.) in which the characteristics of the Athenian state ship on its yearly mission to Delos to honor Apollo have been unified with those of the black boat which sails the Acheron in the Underworld.[84] The play was produced in 467 B.C.—very close in time to the painting of the Cnidian Lesche. Perhaps, then, the representation of the dark ship which ferried the dead across the Acheron in Polygnotus' *Nekyia* (Paus. 10.28.1ff.) had some symbolic connection with the state ship of Athens. In that boat, Polygnotus included the figures of Tellis and Cleoboea, both of whom can be related to the artist's homeland of Thasos.[85] Since Polygnotus had strong ties with both Cimon and Athens, the addition to the *Nekyia* of figures associated with his homeland, a member of the Delian League, in a boat symbolically representing the Athenian state ship's mission to the Ionian Apollo on Delos seems not accidental.

Also, there was something else at Delphi which would have helped to reinforce any possible connection between Athens, especially in the person of Cimon, and the paintings. Just inside the entrance to the sacred precinct, Pausanias saw a statue-base commemorating the Athenian victory at Marathon (10.10.1f.). That it was set up primarily through the efforts of Cimon to glorify his family is readily apparent and has been noted elsewhere.[86] The statues on the base were the work of Phidias, who, with Panaenus his brother,[87] had been employed on other projects that can be associated with Cimon (*infra*, pp. 34, 36); the base and its statues seem originally to have stood near the Athenian treasury building,[88] understandable since Pausanias says the funds for both were provided from the spoils of Marathon. Among the "Cimonian" figures on the base were Miltiades, Cimon's father and hero of Marathon; probably Philaeus,[89] namesake of Cimon's family, the Philaids; and Theseus and Acamas. Further evidence that this was primarily a family monument is provided by the figures with which Miltiades is grouped. He is with Athena and Apollo, symbolic representations of the city of Athens and the Delian League—both of which his son, Cimon, headed in the 460's B.C.; also, the figure who may be identified as Philaeus is grouped with two Athenian kings, Theseus and Codrus. The Theseus-Cimon connection is well-known, but Codrus represents more than just another Athenian king. His descendants were traditionally the legendary founders of many of the Ionian cities in the Delian Confederacy.[90] Hence, both groups of figures would reflect the same theme—an inseparable triad of the Philaids, Athens, and the Delian League.[91]

At what point during Cimon's career the monument was erected is not clear; many would place it in the decade of the 460's.[92] Indeed, some would even link it directly to the victory at the Eurymedon.[93] The fact that Cimon's father, Miltiades, appeared with Theseus, Cimon's political figurehead, in a statue group of gods and heroes relevant to Athens and the Delian League, and that Phidias, who can be linked with Cimon's circle,[94] was involved tends to suggest that the monument was a product of Cimon's most prominent years in the mid- 460's B.C. when his power was secure at Athens and he was most active at Delphi. This would be further indicated if Philaeus, the family namesake, were, indeed, another of the statues on the base as suggested. But even if he were not, Cimon did have the motivation to erect a monument like this as soon as he was able. Miltiades, as will be remembered, had been accused of improper conduct in his dealings with Paros, was convicted, and died in humiliation. His son bore the burden of that disgrace, and it was only by using the Delian League as a vehicle that Cimon reestablished himself and his family among the foremost at Athens. Would there have been anyone more interested than Cimon in seeing his father represented so positively in a monument such as this? If Miltiades' inclusion among the statues were only to glorify the battle of Marathon, would not Theseus, whose ghost was traditionally placed at the battle, have done just as well? It was not necessary to introduce a recent historical figure into this com-

pany of gods and heroes. But Miltiades *is* physically represented in the
statue group *with* Theseus—just as the two also appeared in the painting
which depicted Marathon in the Stoa Poikile,[95] a "Cimonian" building.
That mural is associated with Panaenus (*infra*, p. 36), the brother of
Phidias, who, as mentioned above, fashioned the Marathon base. Certainly, the atmosphere in the 450's B.C. would not have been as
favorable for Cimon to raise such a monument—his exile, his decline in
influence, and other factors make the earlier decade much more suitable.
The work would have nicely complemented the dedication to Cimon's
great victory at the Eurymedon (*infra*, p. 28), which certainly must
have been set up soon after the battle (as was, no doubt, the stele which
marked the grave of the Athenian dead at the Eurymedon (Paus.
1.29.14) in Athens).

Whatever the case chronologically, the statue group would have been
erected close to the time when Polygnotus' paintings were first displayed
in the Cnidian Lesche. Two of the figures on the base (three, if Athena is
counted) appear also in the murals—Theseus and his son, Acamas. Since
there was in existence a contemporary monument at Delphi which
grouped Theseus and Acamas with Cimon's family (Miltiades, and probably Philaeus), anyone who saw it could not avoid being reminded of
the link with Cimon if they also viewed the *Iliupersis* and *Nekyia*. This is
not to suggest that the statues on the base were put there specifically to
prompt comparisons with Polygnotus' paintings (they may have been set
up before the murals); but when both monuments had been completed,
such comparisons were unavoidable even to the most casual visitor.

One further observation may be made about the statue group. The
link suggested earlier (*supra*, pp. 7f.) between the two Apollos, Dorian
and Ionian, at the battle of the Eurymedon is physically represented in
the Marathon base. The base was located in the shrine of the Dorian
Apollo, but, portrayed with Athena and Miltiades, the Apollo in the
statue group obviously represented the Ionian Apollo. Hence, there is a
"merging" here of the two Apollos just as when both shared in the victory at the Eurymedon River.

Celebration of Apollo, the Delian League, Athens, Theseus, and
Cimon's family—all of these things are symbolized by the figures on the
Marathon base. The same characteristics have already been postulated
for the paintings in the Cnidian Lesche, paintings by Polygnotus, the
friend of Cimon and also the associate of Phidias (*infra*, p. 34), the man
responsible for sculpting the statues on the base.

It has already been noted that the Athenian treasury originally stood
next to the statue base and that it, too, was reputedly built with funds
from the spoils of Miltiades' victory at Marathon. Since the building's

decoration included representations of Theseus,[96] it also provided another subtle link between Cimon's family and the hero. As the visitor proceeded upward toward the Cnidian Lesche, he would pass the monument to Cimon's triumph at the Eurymedon, a bronze palm with a gilded statue of Athena on it, located north of the parvis of the temple of Apollo.[97] As Gauer has pointed out,[98] Plutarch specifically calls the statue of Athena on this monument a "Palladium." The Palladium was, by most accounts, the symbol of the fall of Troy and was prominently displayed in Polygnotus' *Iliupersis* (Paus. 10.26.3). With the erection of the Athenian Palladium at Delphi, the fall of the contemporary "Trojans," the Persians, who had made their last great stand at the Eurymedon, was celebrated. It consciously linked Cimon's historical campaigns with the exploits of the ancient heroes of Troy, exploits which were glorified in paint only a short distance away in the Lesche of the Cnidians.

All the above monuments would have been set up during the same general period as the Lesche. Directly or indirectly, they linked Cimon and his family to Theseus, the Delian League, and the Eurymedon. Together they also helped reinforce the role Cimon had played in "freeing" Cnidus, relating him directly to the Lesche and the "Thesean" characters represented in the *Iliupersis* and *Nekyia*.

Finally, a close look at the genealogy of Cimon's family, beginning with Philaeus, proves remarkably revealing when compared with figures in the *Iliupersis* and *Nekyia*. The following abbreviated stemma contains the pertinent relationships:

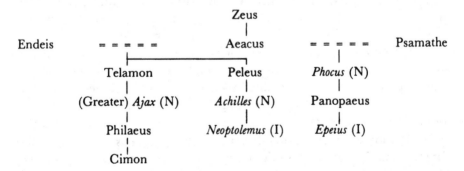

Cimon's family background was indeed rich—his origins going back to a number of prominent heroes and to Zeus himself. Those who appear in either the *Iliupersis* (I) or the *Nekyia* (N) are italicized in the above stemma. The Greater Ajax was Philaeus' father and is pictured in the *Nekyia*; Achilles was the son of Philaeus' grandfather's (Telamon's) brother, Peleus, and is also represented in the *Nekyia*; Achilles' son, Neoptolemus, was the second cousin of Philaeus and appears to have been the most impressive single figure in the *Iliupersis*; Phocus (Paus. 10.30.4), whose presence helped Robert mistakenly conclude that the *Nekyia* had Phocian overtones, was the half-brother of Philaeus' grandfather; and Phocus' grandson, Epeius, fashioner with Athena's help of the Trojan horse and identified by Swindler as one of the most prominent figures in the *Iliupersis*,[99] appears right next to Acamas, Theseus' son, and his friend, Polypoetes (Paus. 10.26.2). Thus, Cimon could legimately claim relationship to five of the most important figures in the two paintings at Delphi.

An argument could be made that Cimon's connection with these figures is purely coincidental and that any family as prominent as his was certain to have a genealogy which contained at least a few of the heroes depicted in the paintings. That might have some merit, but when the figures definitely associated with Cimon's family are added to those which relate to Theseus, Cimon's political figurehead, the list becomes more than impressive:

Cimon's "Relatives"	Theseus-Related
Ajax (N)	Theseus (N)
Achilles (N)	Peirithous (N)
Neoptolemus (I)	Aethra (I)
Phocus (N)	Demophon (I)
Epeius (I)	Acamas (I)
(Epeius' sister, Aegle, though not	Laodice (I)
pictured, was the lover of Theseus	Polypoetes (I)
for whom he left Ariadne)	Ariadne (N)
	Phaedra (N)

Since, as Connor points out, Pherecydes, the Athenian genealogist, published a work—near the time of the paintings—tracing Cimon's ancestry back to Zeus,[100] the connection between the Athenian general and the figures in the murals would not have been lost on the knowledgeable viewer.

A final point is in order before moving on. Some might understandably question placing the *Iliupersis* at Delphi chronologically before the one at Athens, as has been done here. They would argue that there is really no conclusive way to determine which came first and that the mural in the Cnidian Lesche could just as easily be an elaboration of the painting in the Stoa Poikile. Meiggs,[101] for example, thinks that it was not until after the ostracism of Cimon that Polygnotus painted for the Cnidians; nothing more is heard of him in Athens, and, eventually, he returned to his native Thasos, where he held office soon after the middle of the century. The paintings in the Lesche represent the climax of his career. This idea, which has many advocates besides Meiggs,[102] cannot be supported. For one thing, it implies that an artist's best work necessarily comes at the end of his career, which, certainly, has never been demonstrated as a truism. Also, though somewhat dependent upon Cimon, Polygnotus was himself an Athenian citizen, made so as a result of his artistic work. It cannot be assumed that he left when Cimon fell into disfavor, just as it cannot be assumed that Athenian politicians did not tolerate artists who were formerly associated with political enemies. Phidias, for example, worked on Cimonian projects (as did his brother) before becoming closely aligned with Pericles; Ion of Chios, also one of Cimon's circle, was even hostile toward Pericles and yet he continued to produce tragedies in Athens.[103] There is really nothing specific to indicate that it was a change in political climate that led Polygnotus to Delphi and, eventually, back to his native Thasos. In fact, there were Polygnotean paintings in the Periclean Propylaea on the Acropolis. They may have been collected from other places and deposited there, but they could also have been painted by Polygnotus while Pericles ruled Athens.[104] There is no convincing reason for postulating that the *Iliupersis* and *Nekyia* were post-Cimonian. It would also be difficult to understand why Polygnotus would have "packed up his paints" after completing his most famous works. He would have been more in demand than ever, and it is hard to comprehend how, at the height of his career, an artist, from a family of artists,[105] could put down his brushes to become a politician at Thasos.

Happily, there is a very simple solution to the question of the paintings' sequence, and its supports the priority of the Delphic murals. Plutarch, Pliny, and Harpocration all state that Polygnotus did his painting in the Stoa Poikile for free (Plut. *Cim.* 4.6; Plin. *NH* 35.58; and Harp. s.v. "Polygnotus"). It was because of this, Harpocration adds, that Polygnotus was granted Athenian citizenship (though his remarks may be construed to mean that citizenship was awarded for all the artist's work in Athens[106]). To paint without fee must have been an unusual occurrence since all three writers emphasize the point. Pliny makes sure to mention that Polygnotus' fellow artist, Micon, *did* charge for his work in the Stoa, and Plutarch indicates his distaste for "common workmen" who paint for profit, complimenting Polygnotus for his "patriotic zeal." It is not difficult to understand how painting without a fee could be misconstrued by later writers such as Plutarch, who read more idealistic motives into Polygnotus' act than actually existed; even Meiggs has been misled, suggesting that Polygnotus was a "gentleman," who apparently did not have to paint for a living.[107] However, the explanation for

Polygnotus' generosity is not really so difficult to understand, and it has little to do with idealism or personal wealth. Pliny relates that the Amphictyones, which he describes as the "common council of Greece," had decreed free food and lodging for Polygnotus. There is only one Amphictyonic Council to which Pliny could be referring in such a general manner and still be understood—that is the one associated with Delphi. Obviously, free food and lodging had been offered the artist as a result of his great and famous work at Delphi. Consequently, Polygnotus had no reason to charge for his later paintings in Athens since that city was a member of the Council[108] and, therefore, was already contributing to his upkeep. Polygnotus could afford to paint without fee, unlike Micon and others, who were not in as fortunate a situation. Add whatever Polygnotus received "in appreciation" from Cimon, and he must have been making a fair living. Patriotic zeal had nothing to do with it. A wealthy, gentleman artist, who painted on a grand scale while looking for political patronage would certainly be a rarity not just in this age, but in any age; and, if there were such a man, a decree of the Amphictyonic Council for free food and lodging would not have had much meaning since Polygnotus could have provided same with small effort. The Council's gesture has more the ring of the type of honor paid prominent athletes in antiquity who traded their skills for maintenance at their city's expense. That is exactly what Polygnotus seemed to be doing in Athens. Thus, the Council's decree would have to have been in effect before Polygnotus did his "free" painting in Athens—and that means the work at Delphi had already been completed. The sequence of paintings, then, can be established on relatively firm ground.

It has become apparent how often Cimon's path crossed that of the Cnidians. He spent time at Cnidus preparing for the Eurymedon and, therefore, would have been personally known to at least the most prominent Cnidians; he led them and other Greeks in the battle itself, so more Cnidians knew him as their commander; he defeated the Persians at the Eurymedon and would have been viewed as Apollo's "agent" by Cnidians; he remained their leader as head of the Delian Confederation, and his philo-Lacedaemonian attitudes probably would have held him in fine stead with Dorian Cnidus until relations between Athens and member-states of the League began to sour in the later 460's B.C.; he, too, as the leader of one of the most important states of the Amphictyonic Council, was active and prominent at Delphi during the same period the Cnidians would have been building their Lesche. Two monuments at the shrine can be *directly* related to him—the Marathon base and the Athenian dedication to the victory at the Eurymedon—another, the Athenian treasury, may at least be associated with his family. These points plus the details in the *Iliupersis* and *Nekyia* which can be taken to represent a pro-Cimonian sentiment have strongly indicated a connection between Cimon and the Cnidian Lesche, a contention which seems assured by the fact that Cimon was also closely associated with the artist the Cnidians chose to paint the murals in their building—Polygnotus.

CHAPTER THREE

CIMON AND POLYGNOTUS

Polygnotus recognized Cimon as his patron[109] and was the first known artistic advisor to an Athenian politician.[110] Cimon recognized the advantages of surrounding himself with famous artists, poets, and writers. Among the members of his circle, the names of Pindar,[111] Ion of Chios,[112] Melanthius,[113] Archelaus,[114] Phidias and his brother, Panaenus (*infra*, pp. 34, 36), and Pherecydes the genealogist[115] can probably be safely included with Polygnotus. Sophocles is also a possibility,[116] and Simonides, even though a friend of Themistocles, Cimon's political enemy, *did* write on Theseus—in fact, he was one of the first Greek poets to treat the hero (e.g. Plut. *Thes.* 10.2; 17.5 (Bergk, frags. 193, 54); see Connor (*infra*, n. 55) 145ff.). This may have pleased Cimon and might also help explain why it was his epigram on the *Iliupersis*. All these men produced works which in some way treated favorably either Cimon or Theseus. Of Cimon's relationship with the above, most is known about his friendship with Polygnotus; undoubtedly, it was Cimon's influence which helped the artist obtain his Athenian citizenship, an honor not frequently extended to foreigners. Polygnotus also attracted the affections of Cimon's free-spirited sister, Elpinice, who became his lover and, as mentioned previously (*supra*, p. 18), whose face he painted for Laodice's in his *Iliupersis* in the Stoa Poikile.

It is tempting to speculate that Polygnotus had become a member of Cimon's circle as a result of the latter's reduction of Thasos for bolting from the Delian League in 465 B.C. Polygnotus was a Thasian and could have been "persuaded" when the revolt was over to enter Cimon's service. However, indications are that the association went back to a much earlier time. An increasing number of scholars favor a simple emendation of Harpocration which would confirm that Polygnotus was, along with Micon, an artist in the Theseum in Athens,[117] the shrine for the bones of Theseus, returned by Cimon from Scyros ca. 476/75 B.C. A recent study by Barron[118] solidly embraces this idea (it suggests, in fact, that he was the major artist in the Theseum), and Meiggs[119] declares that Cimon had become acquainted with Polygnotus during his campaigns at Eion and Scyros, persuading him to come to Athens when he returned with Theseus' bones. An even earlier date for the relationship may be indicated by Pausanias' statement (9.4.1f.) that Polygnotus painted in the sanctuary of Athena *Areia* at Plataea. Pausanias indicates that the sanctuary was built with spoils from Marathon, but Plutarch (*Aristid.* 20.3) connects it with the battle of Plataea in 479 B.C. However, there is some controversy as to whether Plutarch's text should be read that the shrine was "built" (ᾠκοδόμησαν) or "rebuilt" (ἀνῳκοδόμησαν) after Plataea. The latter interpretation certainly seems the more sensible since it would nicely corroborate the statements of both Pausanias and Plutarch. Originally, a shrine of some sort was constructed using funds from the spoils of Marathon, in which the Plataeans had participated; it was destroyed, partially or completely, in the battle of Plataea (after destroying Athens, there is no reason why the Persians would have spared this temple) and was "rebuilt" with the booty from that conflict. It was in this latter version of the temple which dates from shortly after 479 B.C.[120] that Polygnotus did his painting. His murals could have been added later, but the early date of the building makes it a prime candidate for some of Polygnotus' first important work. As Meiggs has observed,[121] Plataea had a special relationship with Athens. Since the tradition Pausanias relates ties the sanctuary with Marathon, and since Miltiades, Cimon's father, was the hero of that battle, some connection between Cimon and the shrine may be postulated. In fact, one might expect Cimon to take an active part in any restoration or rebuilding of a sanctuary for which his father's victory was responsible. Perhaps this is why Polygnotus was chosen to paint the murals here, and the fact that he did may be the earliest indication of his association with Cimon. Such a suggestion is well within the realm of possibility since Phidias, who fashioned the statues of the Marathon base, was also at work in the same sanctuary.[122] He made the cult statue of Athena for the temple. Consequently, two artists who would be linked with Cimonian projects in the future were working together in a building which was at least indirectly tied to Miltiades.

It seems certain that by the time the Cnidian Lesche was commissioned, Polygnotus was already a member of Cimon's circle. He would have been a well-known artist, who had a reputation as an innovator (Plin. *NH* 35.58), and other painters would have been already imitating his style (Ael. *VH* 4.3). But it really was not until he had done his work in the Lesche that his reputation as the greatest of all Greek mural painters was assured. He was certainly prominent before that time but may not have been much more famous than his contemporary, Micon, with whom he shared painting duties in more than one building in which Cimon's influence can be detected.[123] What, then, would have prompted the Cnidians to choose Polygnotus over other famous artists of the day? No connection between Cnidus and Polygnotus can be theorized to explain the choice, but there *was* a connection between Cimon and

Polygnotus, and the former's influence with both the Cnidians and Delphians has already been noted. It seems natural to suggest that it was these connections which were mainly responsible for the Cnidians' selection of Polygnotus.

Polygnotus would paint, or had already painted, a number of themes in public buildings which related, like those in the Cnidian Lesche, to the "Trojan Cycle." In the sanctuary of Athena *Areia* at Plataea (Paus. 9.4.1), he represented Odysseus, after having slain the suitors—the act had been completed just as he represented Troy *after* its fall in the *Iliupersis*; in the Periclean Propylaea in Athens was his mural of Odysseus encountering the girls who were washing with Nausicaa (Paus. 1.22.6) as it was described by Homer; there, too, was Achilles dwelling among the virgins at Scyros. Clearly, the Trojan War and its heroes were always a major preoccupation of the artist.

It is also clear that Polygnotus was employed for the Cnidian Lesche in much the same manner that he and fellow artist, Micon, were employed by Cimon in Athenian buildings connected with the latter—the Theseum, the Anakeion, and the Stoa Poikile.[124] In the Theseum,[125] Polygnotus (*supra*, p. 33) and Micon[126] painted murals which glorified the highlights of Theseus' life and indirectly reflected upon Cimon. The Anakeion, or sanctuary of the Dioscuri,[127] cannot be dated precisely, but since the traditional account made the duo honorary citizens of Athens, it is likely that some sort of shrine had been erected in their honor before the Persian Wars. In that case, it certainly would have suffered partial or complete destruction when Athens was burned to the ground in 479 B.C. Cimon's pro-Lacedaemonian feelings and his well-known desire to foster good relations with Sparta would have made the restoration of this building an important part of his rebuilding program. It was a symbol, like the Theseum, of his political policies since the Dioscuri had their center of worship at Sparta. Polygnotus and Micon[128] were at work here, too, the former painting the marriage of the daughters of Leucippus (Paus. 1.18.1), an incident from the gods' background. The artists were painting pro-Lacedaemonian scenes in a pro-Lacedaemonian building commissioned by the pro-Lacedaemonian Cimon.[129] Finally, there were the paintings in the Stoa Poikile, which might just as well be called a "Cimonian" picture gallery.[130] The Stoa was built by Cimon's brother-in-law (*supra*, p. 19), and the *Iliupersis* Polygnotus painted there has already been shown to have clear connections with Cimon and Theseus (*supra*, pp. 18ff.). But at least two other paintings in this same building, the most important ones besides the *Iliupersis*,[131] also relate to Cimon's family and/or Theseus. There was the *Amazonomachy* (Paus. 1.15.1), similar perhaps to the one in the Theseum, which was dominated by the

figure of Theseus, who, along with his fellow Athenians, is battling back
the woman warriors; and there was the "Battle of Marathon" (Paus.
1.15.1), in which Theseus' ghost is present and Cimon's father,
Miltiades, was a prominent figure.[132] The artists, again, are the old
familiars of Cimon. Micon painted the *Amazonomachy*; the Marathon
painting was done by the same Micon and/or Panaenus,[133] the brother of
Phidias. Polygnotus, of course, did the *Iliupersis*, but he may also have exercised a supervisory capacity over the decoration of the entire
building.[134] Hence, the three major paintings in the Stoa Poikile were
permeated with "Cimonism." Furthermore, all three of these murals
have been linked by others with the Persian Wars, specifically campaigns
in which Cimon's family was involved. L. H. Jeffrey,[135] has tied the
Amazonomachy to the Scyros operation, and Meiggs has stated his belief
that the *Iliupersis* may have been intended to recall Cimon's Persian victories.[136] By implication, this latter suggestion tends to support a major
thesis of this paper—that the *Iliupersis* at Delphi celebrated Cimon's campaigns against the Persians which ended at the Eurymedon—since the
Athenian version of the painting is a reproduction of the one at Delphi.
Boersma goes even further and proposes that both the Stoa and its paintings were probably commissioned in celebration of Cimon's victory at
the Eurymedon.[137]

If the Cnidian Lesche were so much associated with Cimon, why was
there no *direct* reference made to him somewhere on or in the building? It
was a Cnidian dedication, but this would not necessarily be the prime
reason for omitting Cimon's name. It would have been considered improper at this time to specifically mention a living individual's name on a
monument such as this. Thus, Plutarch (*Cim.* 7.3-8.1) says the Athenians
allowed Cimon to set up three Herms in the Agora to honor his victory
over the Persians, but he was nowhere to be mentioned by name—yet
everyone knew the Herms honored his achievements; neither the Athenian monument to the Eurymedon victory nor the Marathon base at
Delphi mention Cimon's name—yet everyone knew he was connected
with both; the Stoa Poikile in Athens contained no reference to
Cimon—yet everyone knew it was built by his brother-in-law and the
paintings within honored him and his family (Aeschines, *In Ctes.* 186,
says Miltiades was not even named in the Marathon painting, yet
everyone knew who he was). There were enough references to Cimon's
ancestors (and Theseus) in the *Iliupersis* and *Nekyia* to make it clear,
whether Cimon were referred to or not, that the Athenian general's exploits were being celebrated. In this respect, the Lesche conforms to all
other "Cimonian" monuments which do not mention his name
specifically but, nonetheless, can be associated with his Persian victories.

CONCLUSION

The Cnidian Lesche and its paintings by Polygnotus were a product of the battle of the Eurymedon. The chronological evidence places it precisely in this period (second quarter of the fifth century B.C.), and there was neither the opportunity nor the money to make such a dedication before that battle, or in the period after the few years directly following it when the Delian Confederacy would have restricted Cnidus' movements and finances. Such a contention is supported by the activities of the Athenian general, Cimon, during the same period. Cimon led the forces of the Delian League at the Eurymedon, and these included the Cnidians. He left from the harbors at Cnidus for the battle and would have been viewed by the Cnidians as the "agent" of both the Dorian and Ionian Apollos. Besides being the "friend" and commander of the Cnidians, Cimon was also very influential at Delphi, and two monuments there celebrate his family, Athens, and the Delian League. The paintings in the Cnidian Lesche reflect a solid pro-Cimonian, pro-Thesean sentiment which was not accidental; and the artist who painted the *Iliupersis* and the *Nekyia* was the personal friend of Cimon and had performed similar tasks for him in several buildings in Athens. Thus, the conclusion seems inescapable that while the Lesche may have been a thank-offering to Apollo by the Cnidians, it was also another of the number of monuments and buildings which celebrated Cimon's conclusion of the wars with Persia—the final event being the great victory at the Eurymedon River.

APPENDICES

APPENDIX I

ON THE GENUINENESS OF
APOLLO'S RESPONSE TO THE CNIDIANS

It is tempting to view the oracle that the Cnidians reportedly received from Apollo and the events which followed with How and Wells (*A Commentary on Herodotus* (Oxford, 1912) 1, 134) as an "excuse for non-resistance" against the Persians. This is also the view recently set forth by J. Fontenrose, *The Delphic Oracle* (Berkeley, 1978) 306. Certainly, the situation lends itself to such an interpretation. Herodotus' sole source for the story was the Cnidians, themselves, and there is no corroborating evidence from Delphi to support their claim that they did, indeed, consult Apollo. Nevertheless, H. W. Parke and D. E. W. Wormell (*The Delphic Oracle* (Oxford, 1956) 1, 141) see no reason to doubt the oracle's genuineness and accept Herodotus' account as generally accurate. The latters' interpretation is the correct one since the objections raised against the episode are hardly overwhelming. Fontenrose considers the injuries sustained by the Cnidian workmen too "suspicious" to be credible. Evidently, he has never hit a rock with a hammer and experienced the result. The Cnidians obviously would have been "throwing caution to the wind" to complete the channel before the Persian arrival; such haste makes the type of injury described by Herodotus—rock splinters in the eyes—not only plausible but practically unavoidable. If there were no sign that such cutting as Herodotus describes was going on, the case might be somewhat weaker, but the isthmus does show traces of the unfinished work (cf. T. A. B. Spratt, "Remarks on the Dorian Peninsula and Gulf," *Archaeologica* 49 (1886) 347ff.; How and Wells, *loc. cit.* and *ATL* 1, 504). Fontenrose also suggests that the Cnidians would not have had time to consult the Oracle at Delphi. Since there is no way to determine how much time they did have before Harpagus' arrival (he was somewhere in Ionia), there is no point in trying to calculate the number of days or weeks the Cnidians did or did not have. Obviously, they thought there was enough time to dig their channel, so there could also have been time to consult Delphi and return. Since it has already been demonstrated that Cnidus enjoyed a favorable relationship with Delphi (*supra*, p. 3), the priests there would have done all they could to facilitate the Cnidians. Oracles can be manipulated and oracular responses fabricated, but there is nothing substantial to suggest that this is one such case. If the Cnidians were pressed for time, it may be that some type of "preliminary sign" from Apollo was obtained from the god's priest at his shrine in Triopium. In the arguments against the acceptance of Herodotus' account, there is little or no reference made to the fact that there was such an important temple to Apollo in Cnidian territory. This alone would seem to belie the skeptics since it seems doubtful that the protectors of a shrine to Apollo who repeatedly demonstrated their dedication to the god at Delphi would be making up oracles and jeopardizing their good relations with the god and the other cities that used the temple at Triopium (*supra*, p. 3, n. 8). Herodotus (1.144) says that Halicarnassus was barred from using the local shrine simply because one of its citizens committed a minor religious offense against the god. Whether or not this was the true reason (cf. How and Wells, 1, 121), it still is indication of how seriously even a minor blasphemy would be regarded. A sacrilege as serious as fabricating an oracular response was certain to have dire consequences. Also, Herodotus was writing in the 450's B.C. which means that the story about the oracle had to have been circulating earlier during the same era that the Lesche and its paintings were being set up at Delphi. It is doubtful that the Delphians would have been so receptive—despite the magnificence of the gift—to a people who were going about recounting a false Delphic oracle about themselves. There must, therefore, have been some knowledge of the Cnidians' visit to the shrine, and, as Parke and Wormell have suggested, it was not recorded at Delphi because it "contained nothing for Delphi to record with pride, while the local traditions of Cnidus might well preserve it as significant (141)." Cf. also Bean (*infra*, n. 6) 137.

APPENDIX II

SHIP MODIFICATIONS AT CNIDUS

Plutarch's text (Teubner) at *Cimon* 12.2 reads as follows:

. . . πυθόμενος δὲ τοὺς βασιλέως στρατηγοὺς με- 2
γάλῳ στρατῷ καὶ ναυσὶ πολλαῖς ἐφεδρεύειν περὶ Παμφυ-
20 λίαν, καὶ βουλόμενος αὐτοῖς ἄπλουν καὶ ἀνέμβατον ὅλως 486
ὑπὸ φόβου τὴν ἐντὸς Χελιδονίων ποιήσασθαι θάλατταν,
ὥρμησεν ἄρας ἀπὸ Κνίδου καὶ Τριοπίου τριακοσίμις τριή-
ρεσι, πρὸς μὲν τάχος ἀπ' ἀρχῆς καὶ περιαγωγὴν ὑπὸ
Θεμιστοκλέους ἄριστα κατεσκευασμέναις, ἐκεῖνος δὲ τότε
25 καὶ πλατυτέρας ἐποίησεν αὐτάς, καὶ διάβασιν τοῖς κατα-
στρώμασιν ἔδωκεν, ὡς ἂν ὑπὸ πολλῶν ὁπλιτῶν μαχιμώ-
τεραι προσφέροιντο τοῖς πολεμίοις.   3

Δ   τρια   22 τρια-
χοσίαις S: τριαχοσίαις U διαχοσίαις A (διαχοσίας Diod.; cf. 18, 1)

It would appear to indicate that the ship modifications of which Plutarch
speaks were carried out at Cnidus. This seems verified by the context in
which the passage occurs. First, Cimon sails with his fleet of 300 triremes
from Cnidus; then Plutarch mentions that these ships had been built by
Themistocles for speed and maneuverability, but that Cimon now
widened them and built bridges between the decks so that the hoplites
they carried could fight more effectively; Cimon's difficulties with the
Phaselians follow immediately, and then the battle at the Eurymedon.
The modifications, therefore, seem to be an integral part of the narrative
developing the events leading up to the Eurymedon. The text does not
imply that these modifications had taken place earlier as Meiggs (*infra*, n.
19) 76, seems to be suggesting, and, if they did not relate directly to
Cnidus, why would Plutarch wait until precisely this point in his narrative to bring it up? It would have been much more appropriate to mention the modifications while Cimon was raiding the coast of Asia Minor,
or during the great battle of the Eurymedon, itself, when their effects
would have been felt most.

Some might argue that Plutarch here is not talking about modifications
at all; instead, he is speaking of an entirely new type of warship which
Cimon had ordered to meet the demands of the naval warfare of his day.
It was this fleet of new warships that arrived at Cnidus and later sailed for
the Eurymedon. However, such an interpretation does not seem likely.
The text certainly does not require it, and, more importantly, it would be
ridiculous to believe that Cimon had a new fleet of 300 triremes. There

must have been some new ships, and their designs may have been slightly different from the older vessels; but simple economics dictates that the greater part of the fleet would have been comprised of the same vessels which had seen action at Salamis and Mycale slightly more than a decade earlier. Thus, it is modifications to which Plutarch is referring—not a new fleet.

There is, however, one argument which would completely eliminate Cnidus as the location for the modifications; that relates to Plutarch's comment about Cimon making his ships "broader" or "wider" in some fashion. Exactly what he means by this is unclear, but if Plutarch is saying that the hulls of the ships were widened, then the work could not possibly have been completed at Cnidus. This cannot be Plutarch's meaning. Widening the hulls of upwards of 300 warships would have kept the shipyards of the Delian League busy for quite some time. Since the fleet was in use a large part of the year and could be called into action at any moment, the work would have to have proceeded in a piecemeal fashion. Furthermore, this would have been a permanent conversion; these ships would now resemble troop transports more than warships. Their speed and maneuverability would be lost forever, and they could be useful only for a specific kind of fighting, totally impractical for sea chases and the like. Plutarch's own account (*Cim.* 12.5f.) of the fleet's performance at the Eurymedon belies such an interpretation since Cimon's ships were able to outmaneuver and overtake enemy vessels with apparent ease. Consequently, Plutarch cannot be referring to a widening of the ships' hulls, a conclusion to which Gomme (*infra*, n. 17) 1, 287, also appeared headed when he expressed his suspicions about just how effective such ships could be in battle.

In a practical sense, the only thing Plutarch can be referring to when he makes his comment about the widening of the ships is the upper part of the vessels. This would make perfect sense, since an extension of the deck surface would be just the thing to enhance the fighting effectiveness of the hoplites; and, at the same time, it would only hamper but not eliminate the ships' speed and ability to maneuver. Such modifications need only be temporary, and Plutarch implies that they were made specifically for the Eurymedon campaign. The ships could later be restored to their original appearance when a more conventional type of warfare was required. Such modifications as these could have been carried out at Cnidus. Cf. B. Jordan, *The Athenian Navy in the Classical Period* (Berkeley, 1975) 189f., who also interprets Plutarch's text to mean only that the breadth of the decks was increased; J. S. Morrison and R. T. Williams, *Greek Oared Ships 900-332 B.C.* (Cambridge, 1968) 162f.; A. J. Podlecki, *The Life of Themistocles* (Montreal, 1975) 204; and F. E. Adcock, *The Greek and Macedonian Art of War* (Berkeley, 1957) 33.

THE THREE "HERMAE"

Aeschines, *In Ctes*. 183ff., repeats almost verbatim the inscription Plutarch (*Cim*. 7.1-8.1) cites as being on the third of the Herms set up in Athens to celebrate Cimon's victory at Eion. That inscription, as well as those which appeared on the other two Herms, have been the subject of much unnecessary controversy. Wade-Gery (*infra*, n. 31) 82ff., following von Domaszewski (*Die Hermen der Agora zu Athen. Sitz. Ber.* (Heidelberg, 1914) Abh. 10, 13ff.), would, for no good reason, discredit Aeschines' version of what was written on the second and third Herms and substitutes for them the two halves of the much-discussed inscription mentioned by Diodorus (11.62.3) on the Eurymedon and Cyprus. By doing this, he believes the three Herms would then conveniently refer to Cimon's successes at Eion, the Eurymedon, and Cyprus, respectively. How did Aeschines make such a mistake? Wade-Gery theorizes that he was quoting his version of the Herm epigrams from a no longer extant "orators' handbook," which was a handy collection of quotable verse inscriptions. Jacoby, "Some Athenian Epigrams from the Persian Wars," *Hesperia* 14 (1945) 185ff., too, finds some problems with Aeschines but of an entirely different nature. He accepts the orator's report of what was written on the three Herms, and that they all celebrated the Eion campaign; however, they have been cited in the wrong order. What was on the third Herm should actually be placed first, followed by what Aeschines said was written on the first and second Herms.

Exercises such as these seem to be pointless. As Wycherley *Agora* (*infra*, n. 50) 3, 104, has already correctly suggested, the Herms were located in a central place, easily accessible and available daily for public scrutiny. There were relatives of those whose accomplishments these Herms glorified as well as others to whom the inscriptions would have been well-known. It seems difficult to believe that Aeschines, if only for the sake of his own reputation, would have committed such a blunder as misquoting the verses on such familiar public monuments; he certainly would have been "called down" for such by his audience and thoroughly embarrassed and discredited. Furthermore, Wade-Gery (89, n. 76) himself feels that Plutarch derived his version of the inscriptions on the Herms from a source other than Aeschines. How, then, if two independent traditions cite almost verbatim the same version of what appeared on the dedications can speculation such as Wade-Gery's and Jacoby's be correct? Cf. also Gomme (*infra*, n. 17) 1, 288; Jeffery (*infra*, n. 50) 45, n. 19; J. Barns, "Cimon and the First Athenian Expedition to Cyprus," *Historia* 2 (1953-54) 167ff.; and Gauer (*infra*, n. 31) 15, and n. 23.

TELLIS AND CLEOBOEA

It seems clear that Polygnotus inserted Tellis and Cleoboea into the painting to glorify Thasos. They were important in the early tradition of his homeland but were not very well-known elsewhere as is clear from Pausanias. All he knew was that Tellis was the grandfather of Archilochus, the poet, and that Cleoboea was the one who brought the sacred rites of Demeter to Thasos from Paros (10.28.3). Polygnotus might somehow have meant the latter to be connected with the celebration of the Eleusinian Mysteries at Athens. He included Tellis because he was the founder of Thasos. Tellis, like Cleoboea, was from Paros. Besides representing Tellis in the painting, Polygnotus followed the account of his grandson, Archilochus, in depicting Tantalus in the *Nekyia* (Paus. 10.31.12). It is apparent that the artist was deeply influenced by the traditional stories and figures associated with his home. Since Tellis, Cleoboea, and Archilochus are all connected with Paros, perhaps this is an indication that Polygnotus traced his own ancestry back to the original foundation of Thasos (he appears to have come from a prominent family of artists, who were involved in the government of Thasos (*supra*, pp. 29f.)) and believed these figures were somehow related to him. Cf. also Robertson (*infra*, n. 1) 1, 266f.; and Lesky (*infra*, n. 42) 109f.

There may also be another reason for Cleoboea's presence in the *Nekyia*. It, again, relates to the cult of Demeter which she traditionally brought to Thasos from Paros. Herodotus (6.134f.) recounts what he calls a story which the Parians alone tell. According to their testimony, when Miltiades, Cimon's father, was unable to subdue Paros, he intended to desecrate the shrine of Demeter. Alone, he leaped over the precinct wall, and, having reached the door, a feeling of horror came over him. He turned back and fled, hurting his leg in the process. Miltiades would, of course, later die from a leg wound which he received on Paros, so the above story implied that it was Demeter who had ultimately punished Miltiades for disturbing her sanctuary. This tradition was even tied to Delphi because the Parians sent a delegation there to inquire about what to do with a priestess of the temple who advised Miltiades to commit his sacrilege. They were told that she was only luring Miltiades to his destruction, which was all part of a divine plan. Consequently, there was a minor story circulating which connected Miltiades unflatteringly to the cult of Demeter on Paros, which had been brought to Thasos by

Cleoboea. The situation is not unlike that of the Lesser Ajax, who had violated Athena's shrine and was pictured trying to make amends (though unsuccessfully as his situation in the *Nekyia* shows) in the *Iliupersis*. Does Cleoboea's presence in this painting relate in any way to the tradition Herodotus mentions; or, as stated earlier, is Polygnotus simply representing her with Tellis as a founder of an important religious cult on Thasos? (Interestingly, Polygnotus represented a man being punished for sacrilege directly beneath the boat of Charon in which Tellis and Cleoboea were situated: Paus. 10.28.5.) It is hard to decide, but if there is a negative reference being made to Miltiades, it is not a result of any pro-Dorian sentiment; it is purely a manifestation of Polygnotus' own personal feelings. It is clear from his personality that he was a rather independent fellow, who, even though closely aligned with Cimon, was not beyond expressing his discontent with the latter's father. The painting was done at about the same time that relations between Athens and Thasos were beginning to deteriorate or already had. Polygnotus might have been reminding Cimon here of what Demeter had done to his father for attacking Paros, the mother city of Thasos, the artist's home, which Cimon would ultimately have to suppress.

SELECT BIBLIOGRAPHY

Amandry, P. "Notes de Topographie et d'Architecture Delphiques, 4. Le palmier de bronze de l'Eurymedon." *BCH* 78 (1954) 295ff.

Barron, J. P. "New Light on Old Walls: The Murals of the Theseion." *JHS* 92 (1972) 20ff.

Bean, G. E. *Turkey Beyond the Maeander* (London, 1971).

——, and Cooke, J. M. "The Cnidia." *ABSA* 47 (1952) 208ff.

Boersma, J. S. "On the Political Background of the Hephaesteion." *Bulletin van de Vereeniging tot Bevordering der Kennis van de Antieke Beschaving* 39 (1964) 101ff.

——. *Athenian Building Policy from 561/0-405/4 B.C.* (Groningen, 1970).

Bourguet, É. *Les ruines de Delphes* (Paris, 1914).

Burchner. "Knidos." *RE* 11^1, 914ff.

Cahn, H. A. *Knidos, die Münzen des sechsten und des fünften Jahrhunderts v. Chr.* (Berlin, 1970).

Connor, W. R. "Theseus in Classical Athens." In *The Quest for Theseus* (New York, 1970) 143ff.

Davies, J. K. *Athenian Propertied Families, 600-300 B.C.* (Oxford, 1971).

Défradas, J. *Les Thèmes de la propagande delphique* (Paris, 1954).

Delvoye, C. "Art et politique à Athènes à l'époque di Cimon." *Le monde grec. Pensée, littérature, histoire, documents. Hommages à Claire Préaux* (1975) 801ff.

Dinsmoor, W. B. "Attic Building Accounts." *AJA* 25 (1921) 118ff.

Donnay, G. "Art et politique dans l'Athènes classique." *GBA* 59 (1962) 5ff.

——. "Pindare et Cimon, Thème et contenu politique du premier dithyrambe en l'honneur d'Athènes." *RBPH* 42 (1964) 205f.

——. "Allusions politiques dans l'art attique du Ve siècle." *Revue de l'Université de Bruxelles.* N.S. 19 (1966-67) 244ff.

Dugas, C. "A la lesche des Cnidiens." *REG* 51 (1938) 53ff.

Fornari, F. "Studi Polignotei." *Ausonia* 9 (1919) 93ff.

Forrest, W. G. "Themistocles and Argos." *CQ* N.S. 10 (1960) 221ff.

Frazer, J. G. *Pausanias' Description of Greece* (London, 1898) Vol. 5.

Gauer, W. *Weihgeschenke aus den Perserkriegen* (Tübingen, 1968) *Istanbuler Mitteilungen*. Beiheft 2.

Gomme, A. W. *A Historical Commentary on Thucydides* (Oxford, 1945) Vol. 1.

Harrison, E. B. "The South Frieze of the Nike Temple and the Marathon Painting in the Painted Stoa." *AJA* 76 (1972) 390ff.

Hausmann, U. "Akropolisscherben und Eurymedonkämpfe." *Charites. Studien zur Altertumswissenschaft* (Bonn, 1959) 144ff.

Hölscher, T. *Griechische Historienbilder des 5. und 4. Jahrhunderts v. Chr.* (Würzburg, 1973).

Howe, T. "Sophocles, Mikon and the Argonauts." *AJA* 61 (1957) 341ff.

Jacoby, F. "Some Remarks on Ion of Chios." *CQ* 41 (1947) 1ff.

——. *Atthis, The Local Chronicles of Athens* (Oxford, 1949).

Jeffery, L. H. "The *Battle of Oinoe* in the Stoa Poikile: A Problem in Greek Art and History." *BSA* 60 (1965) 41ff.

Klein, W. *Geschichte der Griechischen Kunst* (Leipzig, 1904) Vol. 1.

Kluwe, D. "Das Marathonweihgeschenk in Delphi—eine Staatsweihung oder Privatweihung des Kimon." *Wiss. Zs. der Friedrich-Schiller Univ. Jena, Ges. u. Sprachwiss. R.* 14 (1965) 21ff.

Kluwe, E. "Das Perikleische Kongressdekret, das Todesjahr des Kimon und seine Bedeutung für die Einordnung der Miltiadesgruppe in Delphi." *Wissenschaftliche Zeitschrift der Universität Rostock* 17 (1968) 677ff.

——. "Studien zur grossen 'ehernen' Athena des Phidias." *Die Krise der griechischen Polis. Dt. Akad. der Wiss. zu Berlin Schr. der Sekt. für Altertumswiss.* 55, 1 (1969) 21ff.

Lippold, G. "Polygnotos." *RE* 22², 1630ff.
Lombardo, G. *Cimone* (Rome, 1934).
Löwy, E. *Polygnotos: ein Buch von griechischen Malerei* (Vienna, 1929).
Méautis, G. "Eschyle et Polygnote." *Revue Archéologique* 10 (1937) 170ff.
Meiggs, R. *The Athenian Empire* (Oxford, 1972).
Meritt, B. D., *et al. The Athenian Tribute Lists*, Vol. 3.
Meritt, L. S., "The Stoa Poikile." *Hesperia* 39 (1970) 248ff.
Molle, A. *Étude de l'iconographie de Thesée en relation avec la politique de Cimon* (1968).
Morgan, C. H. "Pheidias and Olympia." *Hesperia* 21 (1952) 319f.
Pellegrini, G. "The Paintings of Panaenus and the Throne of Zeus at Olympia." *Atti del reale Istituto Veneto di scienze, lettere ed arte* 74 (1915) 1555ff.
Picard, Ch. "De l' 'Ilioupersis' de la lesché delphique aux métopes nord du Parthenon." *REG* 50 (1937) 175ff.
Podlecki, A. J. "Cimon, Skyros and 'Theseus' Bones'." *JHS* 91 (1971) 141ff.
Pouilloux, J. *Fouilles de Delphes* 2, pt. 7. *La Région nord du Sanctuaire* (1960).
Poulsen, F. *Delphi* (London, 1920).
Raubitschek, A. E. "The Inscription on the Base of the Athena Promachus Statue." *AJA* 44 (1940) 109.
——, and Stevens, G. P. "The Pedestal of Athena Promachus." *Hesperia* 15 (1946) 107ff.
——. *Dedications from the Athenian Acropolis* (Cambridge, 1949).
——. "Zu den zwei attischen Marathondenkmälern in Delphi." *Mélanges helléniques offerts à Georges Daux*, 315f.
Robert, C. *Die Nekyia des Polygnot. Hallisches Winckelmannsprogram* (1892).
——. *Die Iliupersis des Polygnot. Hallisches Winckelmannsprogram* (1893).
——. *Die Marathonschlacht in der Poikile. Hallisches Winckelmannsprogram* (1895).
Robertson, M. "The Hero with Two Swords." *Journal of the Warburg and Courtauld Institute* 15 (1952) 99f.
——. "The Hero with Two Swords: A Postscript." *Journal of the Warburg and Courtauld Institute* (1965) 316.
——. "Conjectures in Polygnotus' Troy." *BSA* 62 (1967) 5ff.
——. *A History of Greek Art* (Cambridge, 1975) Vol. 1.
Roux, G. "La terrasse d'Attale I a Delphes." *BCH* 76 (1952) 182ff.
Ruge. "Eurymedon." *RE* 6, 1334.
Schreiber, T. *Die Wandbilder des Polygnot in der Halle der Knidier zu Delphi* (Leipzig, 1897).
Schreiner, J. H. "The Battles of 490 B.C." *PCPS* N.S. 16 (1970) 97ff.
Schröder, B. *Zu Mikon's Gemälde der Marathonschlacht in der Stoa Poikile* (1911).
Schweitzer, B. "Der Paris des Polygnot." *Hermes* 64 (1936) 288ff.
Simon, E. "Polygnotan Painting and the Niobid Painter." *AJA* 67 (1963) 43ff.
Six, J. "Mikon's Fourth Picture in the Theseion." *JHS* (1919) 130ff.
Sordi, M. "La vittoria dell'Eurimedonte e le due spedizioni di Cimone a Cipro." *RSA* 1 (1971) 33ff.
Swindler, M. H. *Ancient Painting* (New Haven, 1929).
Swoboda. "Kimon." *RE* 22², 438ff.
Thompson, H. A. "Excavations in the Athenian Agora: 1949." *Hesperia* 19 (1950) 328ff.
von Domaszewski, A. "Das Denkmal des Miltiades in Delphi." *Sitz. Ber. Heid.* 1924/25, Heft. 4, 19f.
Wade-Gery, H. T. "Classical Epigrams and Epitaphs." *JHS* 53 (1933) 97ff.
Walker, E. M. *CAH*, Vol. 5, Chapter 2.
Weickert, C. "Studien zur Kunstgeschichte des V. Jahrhunderts v. Chr., I: Polygnot." *ADAW* 8 (1947) 22ff.
Weizsäcker, P. *Polygnots Gemälde in der Lesche der Knider in Delphi* (1895).
Wycherley, R. E. "The Painted Stoa." *Phoenix* 7 (1953) 20ff.
——. *The Athenian Agora* (Princeton, 1957) Vol. 3.
——. *The Stones of Athens* (Princeton, 1978).

NOTES

[1] For these measurements, see M. Robertson, *A History of Greek Art* (Cambridge, 1975) 1, 247. On the placement of the paintings inside the Lesche, cf. Paus. 10.25.2, 10.28.1; and, e.g. Robertson 1, 248; J. Pouilloux, *Fouilles de Delphes* 2, pt. 7. *La Région nord du Sanctuaire* (1960) 139; Ch. Picard, "De l' "Ilioupersis" de la lesché delphique aux métopes nord du Parthénon," *REG* 50 (1937) 184ff., cf. fig. 3; M. H. Swindler, *Ancient Painting* (New Haven, 1929) 202; F. Poulsen, *Delphi* (London, 1920) 242; and G. Lippold, "Polygnotos," *RE* 22², 1632ff.

[2] Cf. *Die Iliupersis des Polygnot. Hallisches Winckelmannsprogram* (1893); and *Die Nekyia des Polygnot. Hallisches Winckelmannsprogram* (1892). For other early studies, see E. Löwy, *Polygnot: ein Buch von griechischen Malerei* (Vienna, 1929); T. Schreiber, *Die Wandbilder des Polygnot in der Halle der Knidier zu Delphi* (Leipzig, 1897); and P. Weizsäcker, *Polygnots Gemälde in der Lesche der Knider in Delphi* (1895).

[3] See Bibliography.

[4] H. A. Cahn, *Knidos, die Münzen des sechsten und des fünften Jahrhunderts v. Chr.* (Berlin, 1970).

[5] Pausanias (10.11.1) says Triopas founded Cnidus; Diodorus (5.57.6; 61.2) says he landed in the Cnidia and founded Triopium. Together Pausanias and Diodorus probably preserved the tradition to which the Cnidians, themselves, adhered. The fact that the Cnidians included Triopas in a statue group with Apollo cannot be anything but a reference to Triopas' relation to Triopium, where the center of Cnidian worship to Apollo was located (see *infra*, n. 6) and an affirmation of the tradition that made Triopas the grandson of Apollo. Triopium formed a part of the Cnidian state; it was not independent, so Pausanias' reference to Triopas as the founder of Cnidus easily could be interpreted to include also Triopium. However, the Cnidians' acceptance of this tradition does not mean it is historically correct. For other ancient accounts of the foundation, cf. Strab. 14.653; Theocr. 17.68f.; Callim. h. 6.24f.; Steph. Byz. s.v. "Dotium"; *FGrH* 444 F2; *FGrH* 446 F1. See *infra*, n. 14, for additional discussion.

[6] On the cult, see especially Cahn (*supra*, n. 4) 14, 197ff., and 14, n. 58, where a bibliography, ancient and modern, is included on Triopium; G. E. Bean, *Turkey Beyond the Maeander* (London, 1971) 136, 142ff.; and Bean and J. M. Cooke, "The Cnidia," *ABSA* 47 (1952) 208ff.

[7] *Fouilles de Delphes* (*supra*, n. 1) 123.

[8] The temple was shared by four other Dorian cities: Lindus, Ialysus, Camirus, and Cos. According to Herodotus (1.144), Halicarnassus had been excluded because of a religious offense by one of its citizens. The Dorian festival of the "Dorieia" was celebrated here. Since the temple was located in Cnidian territory, Cnidus exercised the greatest authority over the sanctuary. Cf. Cahn (*supra*, n. 4) 14, 197; and Bean (*supra*, n. 6) 136, 143f.

[9] The theories have been discussed by Pouilloux (*supra*, n. 1) 132ff. Cf. also Robertson (*supra*, n. 1) 1, 247; Swindler (*supra*, n. 1) 202; and Poulsen (*supra*, n. 1) 241.

[10] *De def. or.* 6. Cf. also Poulsen (*supra*, n. 1) 242. However, see Pouilloux (*supra*, n. 1) 134, who says that "... la lesché ne servit jamais de salle d'exercises pour les athlètes ...."

[11] See Pouilloux (*supra*, n. 1) 132ff., for the fullest discussion. For earlier views, see J. G. Frazer, *Pausanias' Description of Greece* (London, 1898) 5, 356f.; É. Bourguet, *Les ruines de Delphes* (Paris, 1914) 274ff.; and Poulsen (*supra*, n. 1) 241f.

[12] Pouilloux (*supra*, n. 1) 134ff.; cf. also Bean and Cooke (*supra*, n. 6) 210ff.; and Poulsen (*supra*, n. 1) 240f.

[13] Cf. *ATL* 1, 504. For general accounts of the history of this period, see especially Bean (*supra*, n. 6) 136ff.; and Cahn (*supra*, n. 4) 14ff. Cahn includes a summary of Cnidian scholarship up to the time of his writing.

[14] Herodotus (1.174) says that the colonists came from Lacedaemon. This has been questioned because of the Spartans' well-known lack of interest in colonization, and, since there is an Argive tradition of the foundation (e.g. Diod. 5.53.2f.), Bean (*supra*, n. 6) 136, for one, would like to attribute the establishment of Cnidus to Argos. However, Herodotus, being a Halicarnassian, was very familiar with the Cnidians, and, certainly, he was relating what he had been told by them about their origins. They at least must have thought they were descended from the Lacedaemonians. Whatever the case, they were Dorians, and that is all that is pertinent to the present study. See Cahn (*supra*, n. 4) 14; and Ed. Will, *Korinthiaka* (Paris, 1955) 287.

[15] See Appendix I, *supra*, pp. 39f.

[16] Cahn (*supra*, n. 4) 15 and n. 68; 16.

[17] *Commentary on Thucydides* (Oxford, 1945) 1, 289ff.

[18] *ATL* 3, 207ff. Cf. also "Knidos," *RE* 11¹, 920; Cahn (*supra*, n. 4) 16.

[19] R. Meiggs, *The Athenian Empire* (Oxford, 1972) 55f.

[20] For example, *ATL* 3, 207ff. Recently, however, Meiggs (*supra*, n. 19) 56ff., has challenged such arguments, leaving the door open for at least some Cyprian cities to have been original members of the Delian League.

[21] *CAH* 5, 42ff.

[22] There is some confusion in the various texts of Plutarch as to whether Cimon had 200 or 300 triremes. The Teubner text (cited in Appendix II, *supra*, p. 41) and Meiggs (*supra*, n. 19) 77, are followed here. On the harbors at Cnidus and Triopium, see Bean (*supra*, n. 6) 138, 143; Bean and Cooke (*supra*, n. 6) 209f.; and Cahn (*supra*, n. 4) 16f. Cf. also Thuc. 8.35. Walker himself mentions Cimon's use of Cnidus (53) which seems to contradict his observation about the area being entirely in Persian hands (*supra*, p. 6) until the Eurymedon campaign.

[23] Meiggs (*supra*, n. 19) 74, sees some problems with Plutarch's chronology in *Cimon* 12, feeling that he has omitted an interval of time between Cimon's winning of the Asian coastline as far as Pamphylia and his campaign which ended at the Eurymedon. Even so, he does not appear to dispute Plutarch's assertion that it was from Cnidus that Cimon initially set sail for the great battle. See also Bean and Cooke (*supra*, n. 6) 209; Bean (*supra*, n. 6) 138, 143; "Knidos" (*supra*, n. 18) 920; G. Lombardo, *Cimone* (Rome, 1934) 81; and Cahn (*supra*, n. 4) 16.

[24] See Appendix II, *supra*, p. 41.

[25] Bean (*supra*, n. 6) 138, 143, actually refers to Cnidus as Cimon's base.

[26] It would be ridiculous to believe that Cimon only won the harbors for the Delian League right before he left from them for the Eurymedon. A fleet the size of his needed protection, suitable anchorage, constant repairs (ships rot after long periods in the water, if nothing else), and many other services which take time and require the security of a safe haven. There were not many such havens which could accommodate him in the waters he was sailing, and he would have been a poor general indeed if he had not known in advance where his men and his ships could obtain the necessary attention. Cnidus was obviously one of the few places upon which he knew he could depend.

[27] Cf. Robertson (*supra*, n. 1) 1, 242; Pouilloux (*supra*, n. 1) 138f.; Swindler (*supra*, n. 1) 202, n. 20. Cahn (*supra*, n. 4) also seems to be suggesting the same.

[28] The location of Triopium and the temple of Apollo are still a matter of dispute. Bean (*supra*, n. 6) 143, has identified an acropolis above the village of Kumyer (cf. also W. Penfield, *Proceedings of the American Philosophical Society* 101 (1957) 393ff.) in the region of Betçe as that of Triopium, and this was probably where the temple was situated. Cf. also Bean and Cooke (*supra*, n. 6) 209 and n. 25. Cahn (*supra*, n. 4) 10ff., 14, 222, however, is unconvinced. It seems certain, though, that wherever along the coast Triopium was located (there is also a controversy over the location of an "Old Cnidus"), the temple of Apollo was on a high spot overlooking the water in full view of the ships in the harbor. See the location of the temple of Apollo Karneios at Cnidus, *AJA* 73 (1969) 218; 74 (1970) 150f.; 77 (1973) 414. Recent archaeological reports on Cnidus (1968 +) appear in *AJA*, *Anatolian Studies*, and *Türk Archeologi Dergisi*.

[29] Pouilloux (*supra*, n. 1) 134ff.

[30a] While Pausanias links this building with the Peloponnesian War (10.11.6), it has now been dated to Xerxes' campaign: cf. P. Amandry, *La colonne des Naxiens et le portique des Athéniens* (Paris, 1953), followed by E. Meyer in his notes added to his translation of Pausanias (Zürich, 1967) 702.

[30b] On the amount of spoils, see Plut. *Cim*. 13.6f., *Per*. 9.4; and Diod. 11.61.7; 62.1ff. On its use in Athens, cf., e.g. C. Delvoye, "Art et politique à Athènes à l'époque di Cimon," *Le monde grec. Pensée, littérature, histoire, documents. Hommages à Claire Préaux* (1975) 801ff.; J. S. Boersma, "On the Political Background of the Hephaesteion," *Bulletin van de Vereeniging tot Bevordering der Kennis van de Antieke Beschaving* 39 (1964) 103ff.; and *Athenian Building Policy from 561/0-405/4 B.C.* (Groningen, 1970) 42ff.; G. Donnay, "Allusions politiques dans l'art attique du Ve siècle," *Revue de l'Université de Bruxelles*, N.S. 19 (1966-67) 248ff.; and "Art et politique dans l'Athènes classique," *GBA* 59 (1962) 5ff. See *infra*, n. 67, for more references.

[31] Cf. H. T. Wade-Gery, "Classical Epigrams and Epitaphs," *JHS* 53 (1933) 97ff.; W. Gauer, *Weihgeschenke aus den Perserkriegen* (Tübingen, 1968). *Istanbuler Mitteilungen*, Beiheft 2, 124.; U. Hausmann, "Akropolisscherben und Eurymedonkämpfe," *Charites. Studien zur Altertumswissenschaft* (Bonn, 1959) 148ff.; and Gomme (*supra*, n. 17) 1, 289.

[32] Ships are suggested by Meritt, *et al.*, *ATL* 3, 242.

[33] Cf. *ATL* 3, 239f., where it states that at least two islands, Thasos and Naxos, are known to have converted from ships to money between 478/77-454 B.C. There must have been others who did the same, and Cnidus may have been one of them.

[34] Meritt, *et al.*, *ATL* 3, 24, originally made Cnidus' tribute to be three talents for 454/53 B.C.; Meiggs (*supra*, n. 19) 524ff., 554, makes it to be five talents for 449 B.C., reduced to three in the late 440's B.C. Cnidus' assessment was far below that of some Carian cities, but well above a number of others. It was in what might be described as a middle range of payment for the area. The fact that Cnidus was not included in the highest assessment bracket for Caria and that its assessment was later reduced could be taken as signs of Cnidus' inability to make its payments; but, obviously, there could be many other reasons, all unknown, to explain the figures. Cf. also Cahn (*supra*, n. 4) 16 and n. 71; and Bean (*supra*, n. 6) 138.

[35] There are dozens of studies. For a few, see Meiggs (*supra*, n. 19) 75ff.; M. Sordi, *RSA* 1 (1971) 33ff.; W. K. Pritchett, *Historia* 18 (1969) 18; N. G. L. Hammond, *JHS* 87 (1967) 41ff.; J. D. Smart, *JHS* 87 (1967) 136ff.; M. E. White, *JHS* 84 (1964) 140ff.; Delvoye (*supra*, n. 30b) 802; F. Frost, *Plutarch's Themistocles, A Historical Commentary* (Princeton, 1980) 191; Lombardo (*supra*, n. 23) 79ff., 139; Gomme (*supra*, n. 17) 1, 286ff.; Walker (*supra*, n. 21) 53ff.; Ed. Meyer, *Gesch. d. Altertums* 4, 1.496ff.; Swindler (*supra*, n. 1) 202, n. 20; "Eurymedon," *RE* 6, 1334; and "Kimon," *RE* 22², 445f. Cf. also nn. 36-38, *infra*.

[36] "Some Remarks on Ion of Chios," *CQ* 41 (1947) 3, and n. 1.

[37] *ATL* 3, 160.

[38] E.g. W. G. Forrest, "Themistocles and Argos," *CQ* N.S. 10 (1960) 238; and R. Sealey, *A History of the Greek City States 700-338 B.C.* (Berkeley, 1976) 250.

[39] Meiggs (*supra*, n. 19) 81f.

[40] Cf. Forrest (*supra*, n. 38) *loc. cit.*

[41] Forrest (*supra*, n. 38) *loc. cit.*, sees political overtones in the "inexperienced" Sophocles' victory over the seasoned Aeschylus, whom he views as an associate of Themistocles (236) and, thereby, an attractive target for Cimon. Awarding the judgment to Sophocles was, therefore, a political maneuver to further discredit the name of the recently-disgraced Themistocles. Whether the incident can be viewed in such blatant political terms is questionable, but it should be noted that in later years there would be a portrait of Sophocles in the Stoa Poikile, a "Cimonian" building (*supra*, pp. 19f., 35f.), and the playwright would be definitely associated with two members of Cimon's circle of friends (*infra*, n. 116). Jacoby (*supra*, n. 36) 3, however, says that we are not told anywhere that Sophocles was on friendly terms with Cimon and calls Aeschylus' defeat "surprising" since he "ruled the stage." Delvoye (*supra*, n. 30b) 807, provides another interesting observation, offering that perhaps Sophocles presented his lost play, *Theseus*, on this occasion and won Cimon's approval because of its pro-Thesean tone.

[42] Aeschylus appears to have made two visits to Sicily, the first before his competition with Sophocles. Plutarch is definitely referring to the second trip, which can hardly have taken place before the production of the *Oresteia* in 458 B.C.—Aeschylus would die in Gela in 456 B.C. Plutarch's explanation of Aeschylus' departure is universally rejected. For the chronology, see, e.g. A. Lesky, *A History of Greek Literature* (New York, 1966) 242f.; "Aischylos," *Der Kleine Pauly*, 192; and "Aeschylus," *OCD*, 17f.

[43] See Forrest (*supra*, n. 38) 238, where he says that "No Athenian, whatever his politics, could fail to be moved" by the victory at the Eurymedon, Athens' and Cimon's "greatest triumph." Professor Janssen advises that Apsephion, by conferring this honor on Cimon and the others, seems to have assumed a task formerly due the polemarch. This might be further support for the idea that the honor was the result of a military victory.

[44] Robertson (*supra*, n. 1) 1, 242, has recently accepted the epigram as Simonides', with qualifications; C. H. Morgan, "Pheidias and Olympia," *Hesperia* 21 (1952) 319f., accepts it, as does Poulsen (*supra*, n. 1) 242; Frazer (*supra*, n. 11) 5, 372, too, considered it the work of Simonides. Negative opinions come from, e.g. Robert, *Nekyia* (*supra*, n. 2) 76, and *Die Marathonschlacht in der Poikile. Hallisches Winckelmannsprogram* (1895) 70ff.; A. Hauvette-Besnault, *De l'authenticité des épigrammes de Simonide* (Paris, 1896) 35f., 137f.; W. Klein, *Gesch. d. Griech. Kunst* (Leipzig, 1904) 1, 437f.; F. Fornari, "Studi Polignotei," *Ausonia* 9 (1919) 113; C. Weickert, "Studien zur Kunstgeschichte des V. Jahrhunderts v. Chr., I: Polygnot," *ADAW* 8 (1947) 22f.; Lippold (*supra*, n. 1) 1634; and now D. Page, *Further Greek Epigrams* (1981) 274, who suggests that Polygnotus himself may have composed the "simple couplet."

[45] *Marm. Par.* 73. Cf. Lesky (*supra*, n. 42) 185.

[46] See Diehl, *Anth. Lyr. Graec.*, "Simonides," 103, 115, 116 (Bergk, *Poet. Lyr. Graec.* "Simonides," 142, 105, 106; Edmonds, *Lyr. Graec.* "Simonides," 171, 132, 133). "Simonides," 103 (Diehl), appears as part of the controversial and much-discussed inscription on the Eurymedon campaign cited by Diodorus (11.62.3). For further discussion on this, see *supra*, p. 15 and n. 52, and especially n. 53.

[47] *Anth. Pal.* 9.758. Cf. Bergk, 162; Hill, *Anth. Lyr.* 152; Edmonds, 192. Simonides was attributed the saying, "Painting is silent poetry; poetry is painting that speaks," so it should not be surprising to find his epigrams on paintings. Plut. *Glor. Ath.* 3. See C. M. Bowra, *Greek Lyric Poetry*[2] (Oxford, 1961) 363.

[48] Robertson (*supra*, n. 1) 1, 242, 244, who believes the epigram on the *Iliupersis* can be Simonides', is also troubled by the lack of a similar verse on the *Nekyia*. His attempt to explain the omission, however, is not convincing.

[49] E.g. cf. Frazer (*supra*, n. 11) 5, 356; and Poulsen (*supra*, n. 1) 239. It is mentioned not only by Pausanias but also by Philostr. *Vit. Apollon.* 6.2.64; and Lucian, *Imag.* 7.

[50] For the ancient testimony, see Synesius, *Epist.* 54, 135. Modern studies include: Robertson (*supra*, n. 1) 1, 244f.; Pouilloux (*supra*, n. 1) 137; G. Roux, "La terrasse d'Attale I a Delphes," *BCH* 76 (1952) 182ff.; J. P. Barron, "New Light on Old Walls: The Murals of the Theseion," *JHS* 92 (1972) 44; L. S. Meritt, "The Stoa Poikile," *Hesperia* 39 (1970) 248ff.; L. H. Jeffery, "The *Battle of Oinoe* in the Stoa Poikile: A Problem in Greek Art and History," *BSA* 60 (1965) 42 and n. 10; Meiggs (*supra*, n. 19) 472; R. E. Wycherley, *The Stones of Athens* (Princeton, 1978) 40, 126f.; *The Athenian Agora* (Princeton, 1957) 3, 44; "The Painted Stoa," *Phoenix* 7 (1953) 20ff.; H. A. Thompson, "Excavations in the Athenian Agora: 1949," *Hesperia* 19 (1950) 328f.; Swindler (*supra*, n. 1) 424, n. 14a; Delvoye (*supra*, n. 30b) 804; Boersma, *Athenian Building Policy* (*supra*, n. 30b) 57; and W. B. Dinsmoor, *Architecture of Ancient Greece*[3] (New York, 1950) 198.

[51] On the Vivenzio hydria (Naples 2422; *FR*, p. 34; *ARV*[2] 189, no. 74, and Addenda 1632; Beazley, *Kleophradesmaler*, pl. 27; Pfuhl, *MuZ*, fig. 378; etc.). Cf. also Robertson (*supra*, n. 1) 1, 250ff.

[52] See also Aeschin. *In Ctes.* 183ff.; Dem. *Lept.* 112. In the "Stoa of the Hermes," cf. Wycherley, *Agora* (*supra*, n. 50) 3, 102ff.

[53] See Appendix III, *supra*, pp. 43f.

[54] Plutarch (*Cim.* 13.3) calls it Salamis and Plataea rolled into one. Cf. also Diod. 11.61.7. A. R. Burn, *Persia and the Greeks* (New York, 1962) 560, describes the Eurymedon as "... a second and greater Mycale."

[55] See, e.g. W. R. Connor, "Theseus in Classical Athens," in *The Quest for Theseus* (New York, 1970) 157ff., 166; A. Molle, *Étude de l'iconographie de Thesée en relation avec la politique de Cimon* (1968); A. J. Podlecki, "Cimon, Skyros and 'Theseus' Bones'," *JHS* 91 (1971) 141ff.; Barron (*supra*, n. 50) 20ff.; Delvoye (*supra*, n. 30b) 806f.; etc.

[56] See especially Forrest (*supra*, n. 38) 227, who says that Delphi after the Persian Wars was an aristocratic place and, with the exception of the Stoa, the Athenian dedications and consultations between 479-460 B.C. were all connected with the name Cimon.

[57] Robert, *Nekyia* (*supra*, n. 2) 76.

[58] Frazer (*supra*, n. 11) 5, 360.

[59] Klein (*supra*, n. 44) 1, 437f.

[60] Weickert (*supra*, n. 44) 22f.

[61] C. Dugas, "A la lesche des Cnidiens," *REG* 51 (1938) 53ff.

[62] E.g. Meiggs (*supra*, n. 19) 277, n. 3; Pouilloux (*supra*, n. 1) 138f.; and J. Défradas, *Les Thèmes de la propagande delphique* (Paris, 1954) 153, n. 1.

[63] Pausanias (10.25.7) implies that there may have been another son of Theseus, Melanippus, present in the scene with Demophon and Aethra. Cf. Frazer (*supra*, n. 11) 5, 369.

[64] Robertson (*supra*, n. 1) 1, 250.

[65] For the date, see Meiggs, *Parthenos and Parthenon. Greece and Rome*, suppl. to vol. 10 (1963) 44, who says that buildings in Athens after 462/61 B.C. did not carry private donor's names due to Ephialtes' democratic reforms. The Stoa had originally been called the "Peisianakteion" after its founder, Peisianax (*supra*, p. 19), so it was well under way or completed by the time of Ephialtes' reform. Cf. also, Meiggs, *Athenian Empire* (*supra*, n. 19) 277, 471; Meritt (*supra*, n. 50) 256f.; Jeffery (*supra*, n. 50) 41; Wycherley, *Agora* (*supra*, n. 50) 3, 45, n. 2; *Stones of Athens* (*supra*, n. 50) 38; T.B.L. Webster, *Potter and Patron in Classical Athens* (London, 1972) 85; Boersma, *Building Policy* (*supra*, n. 30b) 55ff.; and others. Perhaps the new dig in the area of the Stoa will uncover materials which can determine the building's date precisely.

[66] Connor (*supra*, n. 55) 163, says that Polygnotus' painting Elpinice's face was a compliment and acknowledged the connection between his work and Cimon, who was a "powerful" and "generous" patron. In addition, he recognizes that the choice of Laodice was not random because of her affair with Theseus' son—"Considering the frequent allusions to the Theseus legend by the house of Cimon such a selection was clever and appropriate." He believes a similar situation is the appearance of Philaeus, the founder of Cimon's family (Philaids), among the statues in the Marathon group at Delphi (*supra*, pp. 25ff.).

[67] See *supra*, n. 30b, and, specifically for the Promachus, cf. W. B. Dinsmoor, "Attic Building Accounts," *AJA* 25 (1921) 129; A. E. Raubitschek, "The Inscription on the Base of the Athena Promachus Statue," *AJA* 44 (1940) 109; and *Dedications from the Athenian Acropolis* (Cambridge, 1949) no. 172, 198ff.; Raubitschek and G. P. Stevens, "The Pedestal of Athena Promachus," *Hesperia* 15 (1946) 107ff. All these works suggest that the statue commemorated or at least related to Cimon's victory at the Eurymedon. E. Kluwe, "Studien zur grossen "ehernen" Athena des Phidias," in *Die Krise der griechischen Polis. Dt. Akad. der Wiss. zu Berlin Schr. der Sekt. für Altertumswiss.* 55, 1 (1969) 21ff., however, argues against this idea. D. Kluwe, "Das Marathonweihgeschenk in Delphi—eine Staatsweihung oder Privatweihung des Kimon," in *Wiss. Zs. der Friedrich-Schiller Univ. Jena, Ges. u. Sprachwiss. R.* 14 (1965) 25, n. 17, provides a list of various scholars' dating of the monument. See also on the Promachus, Gauer (*supra*, n. 31) 103ff.

[68] J. K. Davies, *Athenian Propertied Families, 600-300 B.C.* (Oxford, 1971) 9688 viii. Cf. also, K. J. Beloch, *Gr. Gesch.*² ii. 2.32; Meiggs (*supra*, n. 19) 96, 276, 471; Robertson (*supra*, n. 1) 1, 243; Jeffery (*supra*, n. 50) 42; Webster (*supra*, n. 65) *loc. cit.*; Delvoye (*supra*, n. 30b) 803; Boersma, *Building Policy* (*supra*, n. 30b) 55; etc.

[69] Cf. Meiggs (*supra*, n. 19) 471: "it was appropriate that a Cimonian should be associated with a new public building in the Agora with magnificent paintings;" also, 276. Jeffery (*supra*, n. 50) 42; Barron (*supra*, n. 50) 33, says the Stoa was built *for* Cimon; Robertson (*supra*, n. 1) 1, 242f.; Boersma, *Building Policy* (*supra*, n. 30b) 55f., relates it to

the Eurymedon victory; Delvoye (*supra*, n. 30b) 804, 806; and D. Kluwe (D. Kitzig), *Kimon, das Marathonweihgeschenk in Delphi und die Bilder der Stoa Poikile in Athen* 58ff., 81ff. (1961): unpublished, cited from E. Kluwe, "Das Perikleische Kongressdekret, das Todes-jahr des Kimon und seine Bedeutung für die Einordnung der Miltiadesgruppe in Delphi," *Wissenschaftliche Zeitschrift der Universität Rostock* 17 (1968) 678ff. See also the discussion in T. Hölscher, *Griechische Historienbilder des 5. und 4. Jahrh. v. Chr.* (Würzburg, 1973) 74ff.

[70] Pausanias' text breaks up while he is enumerating the kings. This leaves room for other kings besides those mentioned, e.g. Menestheus, who traditionally led the Athenians at Troy. Jeffery (*supra*, n. 50) 45, n. 18, believes the latter may have at least been present in the Poikile's *Iliupersis*. Robertson, "Considerations in Polygnotus' Troy," *BSA* 62 (1967) 10, thinks that the lacuna in Pausanias allows for the omission of only one other figure in the Delphic painting and that was Diomedes.

[71] Jeffery (*supra*, n. 50) 58, n. 18, specifically includes Acamas in both murals.

[72] Cf. Jeffery (*supra*, n. 50) 45: "... generally assumed two works did not differ greatly in their presentation ...", and her n. 17; also, Webster (*supra*, n. 65) *loc. cit.*; Frazer (*supra*, n. 11) 5, 367; and Swindler (*supra*, n. 1) 211. Robertson (*supra*, n. 70) 6ff., would also include Epeius, who, under the guidance of Athena, fashioned the "Trojan horse," in the central scene of Ajax's oath. He appears just to the right of Acamas and Polypoetes in the Delphic *Iliupersis*. Cf. also Hölscher (*supra*, n. 69) 70.

[73] Along with the scene depicting Neoptolemus. Cf. Robertson (*supra*, n. 1) 1, 250; and (*supra*, n. 70) 10.

[74] Since Peirithous must have appeared with Theseus in an earlier mural in the Theseum in Athens which depicted the battle of the Lapiths and centaurs (Paus. 1.17.2), a painting which might very well be attributed to Polygnotus (e.g. Barron, *supra*, n. 50, 44; and, *supra*, p. 33), the two pictured together in the *Nekyia* would have immediately evoked thoughts about Athens. There was also in the Theseum a painting which related to Theseus and the Underworld (cf. Robertson, *supra*, n. 1, 1, 243, 256). Cimon seems to have found Theseus and Peirithous a useful motif since it can be associated with other buildings which have been attributed to him, e.g. Boersma, "Hephaesteion," (*supra*, n. 30b) 105f., believes the Hephaesteum was planned under a Cimonian building program (though the general did not live to see the structure completed), and H. A. Thompson, "The Sculptural Adornment of the Hephaisteion," *AJA* 66 (1962) 341ff., identifies the figures of Theseus and Peirithous back to back in the west frieze. See also on this, E. B. Harrison, "The South Frieze of the Nike Temple and the Marathon Painting in the Painted Stoa." *AJA* 76 (1972) 353, pl. 73 (figs. 2, 3). It is also interesting that Panaenus, who worked in the Stoa Poikile, a "Cimonian" building (*supra*, pp. 19f.; *supra*, pp. 35f.), painted Theseus and Peirithous on the "barriers" associated with the golden statue of Zeus his brother, Phidias, made at Olympia. On the same barriers, he had also represented the "oath of Ajax." Cf. Paus. 5.11.5f.; also Robertson (*supra*, n. 1) 1, 317; and G. Pellegrini, "The Paintings of Panaenus and the Throne of Zeus at Olympia," *Atti del reale Istituto Veneto di scienze, lettere ed arte* 74 (1915) 1555ff. Cf. also F. A. Gardner, *JHS* 14 (1894) 233; H. G. Evelyn-White, *JHS* 28 (1908) 54f.; C. H. Tyler, *JHS* 30 (1910) 82; and *AJA* 20 (1961) 488.

[75] "Touching" is the word used by Robertson, "The Hero with Two Swords," *Journal of the Warburg and Courtauld Institute* 15 (1952) 99f.; also the "Postscript" in vol. 28 (1965) 316, of the same journal. See also E. Simon's thoughts on the heroes in the Underworld: "Polygnotan Painting and the Niobid Painter," *AJA* 67 (1963) 45, 47.

[76] After the deaths of both their wives, Peirithous had persuaded Theseus to carry off Helen. They swore an oath to help each other in this dangerous pursuit and agreed to draw lots for her when she had been captured; the winner would help the loser carry off another of Zeus' daughters. Theseus won Helen, and, years later, Peirithous reminded his friend of their pact. They visited an oracle of Zeus, who witnessed their oath, and his response was the suggestion that they carry off his daugther, Persephone, wife of Hades. Peirithous liked the idea, but Theseus was outraged. Nonetheless, the former held his friend to his oath, and Theseus dared not refuse to go.

[77] Robertson (*supra*, n. 70) 11.

[78] Some might argue that Achilles' presence in a painting of the Underworld at Delphi was reminder enough of Apollo's role in placing him there; but there were dozens of figures in the painting, all in the Underworld for different reasons, and nothing distinguishes Achilles from the rest. He is not even pictured by himself but in a group which included Agamemnon, Protesilaus, Patroclus, and Antilochus. If Polygnotus were trying to single out Achilles as an example of one who had felt Apollo's wrath, he certainly went about it in a clumsy and ineffective way. It seems clear that this was never his intention.

[79] Poulsen (*supra*, n. 1) 243. Poulsen calls Neoptolemus the chief person in the painting.

[80] Robertson (*supra*, n. 1) 1, 247, 250f.

[81] Pausanias (10.25.7) may be indicating that another of Theseus' sons, Melanippus, was also present in this scene. Cf. Frazer (*supra*, n. 11) 5, 369. For a very negative opinion of Helen in the *Iliupersis*, see G. Méautis, "Eschyle et Polygnote," *Revue Archéologique* 10 (1937) 170ff.

[82] Robertson (*supra*, n. 1) 1, 268.

[83] Robertson (*supra*, n. 1) 1, 248.

[84] Robertson (*supra*, n. 1) 1, 267. For an earlier attempt to find links between the works of Aeschylus and Polygnotus, see Méautis (*supra*, n. 81) 169ff.

[85] See Appendix IV, *supra*, pp. 45f.

[86] See especially D. Kluwe (*supra*, n. 67) 21ff., and (*supra*, n. 69) *loc. cit.*; E. Kluwe (*supra*, n. 69) *loc. cit.*; Connor (*supra*, n. 55) 163f.; and A. von Domaszewski, "Das Denkmal des Militiades in Delphi," *SB Heid.* 1924/25, Heft. 4, 19f. Cf. also Forrest (*supra*, n. 38) 227, n. 4; Picard (*supra*, n. 1) 189, n. 4; and Gauer (*supra*, n. 31) 65ff.

[87] There is some confusion as to whether Panaenus was Phidias' brother or nephew: see Robertson (*supra*, n. 1) 1, 244, 322. This study will refer to him as brother.

[88] See, e.g. Raubitschek, "Zu den zwei attischen Marathondenkmälern in Delphi," in *Mélanges helléniques offerts à Georges Daux*, 315f.

[89] The name of the figure that appears with Theseus and Codrus on the Marathon base (Paus. 10.10.1) has been emended by some to read "Philaeus." Connor (*supra*, n. 55) 163f., calls this an "easy" and "convincing" emendation which is almost surely correct. D. Kluwe (*supra*, n. 67) 21ff., solidly embraces it without question as does E. Kluwe (*supra*, n. 69) 679. See Gauer (*supra*, n. 31) 66 and n. 255, for further discussion.

[90] See Connor (*supra*, n. 55) 163f.; and D. Kluwe (*supra*, n. 67) 23.

[91] As Connor (*supra*, n. 55) 163ff., states, Cimon is not present among the figures for reasons of "good taste;" but the inclusion of Miltiades and Philaeus was just like Polygnotus' putting Elpinice's features on Laodice's face and reveals the true origin and intention of the work, which Connor considers a transparent effort to use myth and religion for purposes of individual, group, or national aggrandizement.

[92] See E. Kluwe (*supra*, n. 69) 683; D. Kluwe (*supra*, n. 67) 25, n. 17, has provided a list of dates proposed by various scholars for the Marathon base. Also, Connor, 160; and E. Vanderpool, "A Monument to the Battle of Marathon," *Hesperia* 35 (1966) 105f.

[93] E.g. von Domaszewski (*supra*, n. 86) *loc. cit.*

[94] Connor (*supra*, n. 55) 170, says Phidias was a supporter of the Theseus myth and paid extravagant praise to Miltiades in this statue group.

[95] D. Kluwe (*supra*, n. 69), *loc. cit.*, says that "... sowohl die Gemälde in der Stoa Poikile als auch die Miltiadesgruppe in Delphi private Auftragswerke des Kimon waren und ihm als wichtige Propagandamittel für seine politischen Ansichten dienten."

[96] See P. de la Coste-Memèliere, *Fouilles de Délphes* 4, pt. 4. *Sculpture du trésor des Atheniens* (1957) 37ff. Cf. also Barron (*supra*, n. 50) 23, and n. 37.

[97] For the monument's location, see P. Amandry, "Notes de Topographie et d'Architecture Delphiques, 4. Le palmier de bronze de l'Eurymedon," *BCH* 78 (1954) 295ff. See also Gauer (*supra*, n. 31) 105ff.; Hausmann (*supra*, n. 31) 150; and Delvoye (*supra*, n. 30b) 805.

[98] Gauer (*supra*, n. 31) 106f. Cf. Plut. *Nic.* 13.3.

[99] Swindler (*supra*, n. 1) 201f. See Robertson's comments on Epeius (*supra*, n. 72) 6ff.

[100] Connor (*supra*, n. 55) 163f. Cf. F. Jacoby, *Atthis, The Local Chronicles of Athens* (Oxford, 1949) 151 and n. 17; 219 and n. 24; 221, 223. Jacoby believes that Pherecydes probably published his work in the first third of the fifth century B.C. He narrated the story of Theseus in detail and may have had "personal reasons" for giving the full pedigree of the Philaid family.

[101] Meiggs (*supra*, n. 19) 277, 573.

[102] Robertson (*supra*, n. 1) 1, 242ff., leans in this direction. Swindler (*supra*, n. 1) 214, describes the *Iliupersis* as Polygnotus' latest and most finished work. Cf. also, J. H. Schreiner, "The Battles of 490 B.C.," *PCPS* N.S. 16 (1970) 97ff.

[103] Plut. *Per.* 5.3; 28.5. Cf. Meiggs (*supra*, n. 19) 275; and Jacoby (*supra*, n. 36) 2ff. Also, *infra*, n. 112.

[104] See Robertson (*supra*, n. 1) 1, 245.

[105] Polygnotus' father and teacher was Aglaophon (Paus. 10.27.4; Harp. s.v. "Polygnotus"; and Quint. *Inst.* 12.10.1ff.). His brother, Aristophon, was also a painter (Plat. *Grg.* 448B and scholiast).

[106] It is doubtful, considering how grudgingly the Athenians gave citizenship to foreigners, that Polygnotus was awarded it only because of his work in the Poikile. Harpocration, himself, states that some writers say he received citizenship for his work in other buildings in Athens. Both explanations are probably correct since the impressiveness of all Polygnotus' paintings together would certainly justify the honor.

[107] Meiggs (*supra*, n. 19) 276f.

[108] See Raubitschek, "The Peace Policy of Pericles," *AJA* 70 (1966) 40ff., for Athens' influence over decisions of the Amphictyones since the end of the Persian Wars.

[109] Meiggs (*supra*, n. 19) 471, specifically uses the word, "patron."

[110] Donnay, "Art et politique" (*supra*, n. 30b) 13.

[111] Cf. Donnay, "Pindare et Cimon, Thème et contenu politique du premier dithyrambe en l'honneur d'Athènes," *RBPH* 42 (1964) 205f., who states that Pindar subverted his poetry to reflect the political themes of Cimonian Athens and the Delian League. Forrest (*supra*, n. 38) 228, 234, says that "Kimon's world was also Pindar's world."

[112] Plut. *Cim.* 5.3, 9.1ff., 16.8: *Per.* 5.3. See Meiggs (*supra*, n. 19) 275; and Jacoby (*supra*, n. 36) 2ff.

[113] Melanthius wrote in honor of Cimon and also Polygnotus (Plut. *Cim.* 4). Robertson (*supra*, n. 1) 1, 243: Melanthius was a "protégé of Cimon's."

[114] Archelaus also wrote favorably about Cimon (Plut. *Cim.* 4).

[115] See *supra*, n. 100, under Jacoby, *Atthis*.

[116] It has already been mentioned that Cimon and his colleagues favored Sophocles over Aeschylus at the Dionysia of 468 B.C. (*supra*, pp. 9ff.). By itself, this means little, but Sophocles would later be represented (most likely in one of the murals rather than an individual portrait) in the Stoa Poikile playing the lyre (*Biogr. Graeci*, ed. Westermann, p. 127). Some believed that this was meant to recall his own performance on the instrument in his play, *Thamyris*, but this was only tradition and there could just as easily be another explanation. Since Sophocles was depicted in what was essentially a Cimonian picture gallery in a posture that was related in some fashion to his craft as a playwright, it might be suggested that his presence here was designed as a reminder of his celebrated triumph over Aeschylus (though Aeschylus himself appears to have been represented in the Marathon painting (Paus. 1.21.2) in the Stoa (*supra*, p. 36)). Whatever the case, Sophocles *is* linked to the artwork in the Stoa and also to two members of Cimon's circle—Ion of Chios, who records his conversations (Athen. 13.603ff.), and Archelaus, to whom Sophocles wrote an elegiac poem. All this together justifies at least suggesting a possible connection with Cimon's group.

[117] Harpocration's text reads: τὰς ἐν τῷ θησαυρῷ καὶ τῷ Ἀνακείῳ γραφάς. Since there was no *monumental treasury* in Athens, θησείῳ is the most appropriate emendation for θησαυρῷ. Cf. also *Suda* s.v. "Polygnotus." For those who support Polygnotus' participation in painting the Theseum, see, e.g. Barron (*supra*, n. 50) 44f.; Meiggs (*supra*, n. 19) 275; Robertson (*supra*, n. 1) 1, 242; Meritt (*supra*, n. 50) 256; Wycherley, *Agora* (*supra*, n.

50) 3, 114; *Stones* (*supra*, n. 50) 64; Boersma, *Building Policy* (*supra*, n. 30b) 51f.; Podlecki (*supra*, n. 55) 143, n. 22; Swindler (*supra*, n. 1) 205, 207; Delvoye (*supra*, n. 30b) 806; Robert, *Marathonschlacht* (*supra*, n. 44) 46ff.; and A. Rumpf, *EAA* 6, 294f.

[118] Barron (*supra*, n. 50) 44f.

[119] Meiggs (*supra*, n. 19) 275.

[120] Cf. Robertson (*supra*, n. 1) 1, 245f.; Swindler (*supra*, n. 1) 213; and Weickert (*supra*, n. 44) 22f. Other dates proposed for the shrine have been catalogued by Kluwe (*supra*, n. 67) 25, n. 17.

[121] Meiggs (*supra*, n. 19) 277. Meiggs says that Polygnotus' painting in the sanctuary was probably due to his association with Athens.

[122] Phidias was said to have begun his career as a painter (Plin. *NH* 35.54), so he had much in common with Polygnotus. Cf. Robertson (*supra*, n. 1) 1, 242, 312.

[123] See Meiggs (*supra*, n. 19) 276; and *supra*, pp. 35f.

[124] See Robertson (*supra*, n. 1) 1, 242f.; Meiggs (*supra*, n. 19) 276, 573; Boersma (*supra*, n. 30b) 51f.; and other references listed in n. 69 (*supra*).

[125] The ancient testimony for the building has been collected by Wycherley, *Agora* (*supra*, n. 50) 3, 113ff.

[126] Cf. J. Six, "Mikon's Fourth Picture in the Theseion," *JHS* (1919) 130ff.

[127] For the ancient testimony, see Wycherley, *Agora* (*supra*, n. 50) 3, 61ff.

[128] Cf. T. Howe, "Sophocles, Mikon and the Argonauts," *AJA* 61 (1957) 341ff.

[129] This, too, is the view of Meiggs (*supra*, n. 19) 276.

[130] For the ancient testimony, see Wycherley, *Agora* (*supra*, n. 50) 3, 31ff.

[131] Pausanias also mentions a fourth picture (1.15.1), depicting the battle of Oenoe, in which Athenians are drawn up against Lacedaemonians at Oenoe in Argive territory. Scholars have had difficulty identifying this battle and when it took place. Jeffery (*supra*, n. 50) 41ff., has discussed the problem in detail. She suggests that the painting represents a mythological theme of the appeal of the Argive, Adrastus, to Theseus (50), thus making it Thesean in character just like the other murals in the Stoa. Her arguments have been supported by Webster (*supra*, n. 65) 86, 88ff.; but see Hölscher (*supra*, n. 69) 68ff. Meiggs (*supra*, n. 19) 96f., 469ff., has recently reviewed the problem, and his summary is the most sober. He correctly argues that this painting was not one of the original murals in the Stoa, but was added later; consequently, it would bear no relation to Cimon or Theseus. However, see Schreiner (*supra*, n. 102) 101ff., who co-ordinates the painting of the battle of Oenoe with the *Amazonomachy* and the *Iliupersis* in the Poikile; but, cf. Wycherley's objections to Schreiner's major thesis in *PCPS* N.S. 18 (1972) 78. See also on Oenoe, Wycherley, *Agora* (*supra*, n. 50) 3, 40; Gomme (*supra*, n. 17) 1, 370, n. 1; and Delvoye (*supra*, n. 30b) 804.

[132] Connor (*supra*, n. 55) 162f., says Miltiades' prominence was surely congenial to Cimon's supporters. At about this same time, the Marathon base, which also connected Miltiades and Theseus, was set up at Delphi (*supra*, pp. 25f.). Also on the Marathon painting, see Harrison (*supra*, n. 74) 353ff.; Robertson (*supra*, n. 1) 1, 187, 243f., 323f.; and Hölscher (*supra*, n. 69) 50ff.; 78ff.

[133] Pausanias (5.11.6) and Pliny (*NH* 35.57) specifically say Panaenus is the painter of the Marathon mural; others such as Aelian (*Nat. Anim.* 7.38), Arrian (*Anab.* 7.13.5), etc., relate Micon to the painting. On the basis of the sources, one artist may not be eliminated in favor of the other; it is not unlikely that both had a hand in the work. See discussion in Wycherley, *Agora* (*supra*, n. 50) 3, 45, n. 3; Jeffery (supra, n. 50) 43, n. 14; Robertson (*supra*, n. 1) 1, 244, 322. Also cf. B. Schröder, *Zu Mikon's Gemälde der Marathonschlacht in der Stoa Poikile* (1911).

[134] Meiggs (*supra*, n. 19) 276, sums it up by saying Polygnotus was the master, Micon, Panaenus, and others his associates, and that his commission in the building was probably Cimonian in inspiration. See also, Wycherley (*supra*, n. 133) *loc. cit.*; and Robertson (*supra*, n. 1) 1, 244.

[135] Jeffery (*supra*, n. 50) 45. See also Connor (*supra*, n. 55) 156f.; Meiggs (*supra*, n. 19) 276; Boersma, "Hephaisteion," (*supra*, n. 30b) 104. Gauer (*supra*, n. 31) 18, says,

however, "Die attische Amazonomachie wurde ... als mythische Analogie zur Marathonschlacht verstanden;" and 19. Hölscher (*supra*, n. 69) warns against making too specific parallels between the mythological content of the paintings and the Persian Wars.

[136] Meiggs (*supra*, n. 19) 276.

[137] Boersma, *Building Policy* (*supra*, n. 30b) 57.

INDEX

Printed in the United States
By Bookmasters